Leadership Secrets of Saint Paul will li[f]
keep going and not give up. Reading it [...]
mission and challenged me to a higher level of thinking.

Joshua Chang
—Principal of the AG Global Group of Companies

LEADERSHIP
SECRETS *of*

Saint Paul

Jeff Caliguire

RIVER
OAK
PUBLISHING

07 06 05 04 03   10 9 8 7 6 5 4 3 2 1

The Leadership Secrets of Saint Paul
ISBN 1-58919-004-1
Copyright © 2003 Jeff Caliguire

Published by RiverOak Publishing,
An Imprint of Cook Communications Ministries
P.O. Box 55388
Tulsa, Oklahoma 74155

CONTENTS

FOREWORD

We were made to achieve.

The mandate to have *dominion*—to learn, master, discover, and create involves part of what it means to be created in God's image. Our drive to produce value and make a difference is deeply woven into the fabric of our being.

However, we do not exist only to accomplish tasks. Instead of being the goal, these tasks are a tool God uses to shape us into the beings He intended us to be, His goal. These tasks are part of the process by which He develops us.

And it's best to be shaped on purpose:

—to find people in your life that you want to emulate;

—to look at what is actually motivating your actions;

—to be aware of your heart, and not simply your resume.

It's important for you as a leader to reflect not just on what you're doing but also on who you're becoming. Jeff Caliguire's *Leadership Secrets of Saint Paul* is written with you in mind. It's designed to help you who are involved in the challenge of leadership to examine not only your strategy but also your values. Jeff's look at the apostle Paul, whose passion, mission, and ideas continue to shape the world, is designed to cause readers to ask questions about which people most influence them as they discover a man who still engages great human minds and thought two millennia after he left the scene.

I hope you don't merely read this book, but that you also reflect, wrestle, and change, because then the lives of all whom you touch will experience change as well.

John Ortberg
South Barrington, Illinois

Introduction

The Leadership Secrets of Saint Paul captures a picture of a special type of leadership. This extraordinary class of leaders, who we are going to call "entrepreneurial leaders," have been especially gifted, called, or compelled to the task of breaking new ground. They envision what might be and courageously set out to upset the status quo. They utilize creative skills to envision, initiate, or boldly expand businesses, ministries, or other ways to help people. Though sometimes taken for "eccentrics" by others who wonder what drives them, these risk-takers create the pathways of opportunity for themselves and possibly countless others.

If you are visionary, this book will provide you with the tools you need to thrive as you turn the dream into reality—and learn and grow and someday even pass this baton to others. If you are a leader in a well-established organization, it will supply principles for you to develop your own entrepreneurial leadership skills or learn how to unlock the entrepreneurial leaders around you.

You may already know this, but simply put—entrepreneurial leadership isn't for the faint of heart. As someone who has founded a Boston church, a sports organization, and a consulting company focused on helping entrepreneurial leaders and their teams succeed; I have experienced both the thrill and the hazards associated with this lifestyle. I have spent much of my adult life seeking the resources for support, ideas, and needed encouragement for this calling. More recently, I've looked for wisdom and inspiration for those brave souls I've had the privilege to consult.

During one particularly challenging moment in my career journey, I happened upon a man who I had heard about almost my entire life. He was a legend in his field, but I had never thought about him in terms of business insights or as an entrepreneurial role model. Yet, as I read back through the highlights of his life, I realized he lived at the heart of a startup venture that faced overwhelming odds. He took a fledgling endeavor into the international arena with no capital and no employees. His venture was minuscule next to the dominant market forces, and he faced tremendous opposition to his plan from both within and without the organization. Dangerous barriers loomed in many of his essential markets. In fact, the competition was intent on killing him—literally. Yet somehow, his plan succeeded.

I didn't hear this leader speak at a workshop or watch his video. I read his story in an unexpected place—the pages of the Bible.

MEET SAINT PAUL—ENTREPRENEURIAL LEADER

Almost two thousand years ago, this man from Tarsus, a coastal town of Asia Minor, helped launch an enterprise that changed the history of the world. In a time before faxes, cell phones, e-mail, the Internet, and even mass printing technology, he dazzled a disinterested market, resulting in raving fans.

How did he succeed? He committed his entire life to his mission, took every opportunity to share his vision, invested in up-and-coming leaders, and endured when most others would have thrown in the towel. The rest is history.

Before he was Paul, he was called Saul. At the time of his dramatic conversion and subsequent name change, there was only a tiny handful of followers of this divergent religious sect known as the Way. For the most part, its members were poor Jewish peasants with little influence and little access to the power of the non-Jewish majority of the day—the Gentiles. Yet, after a life-altering encounter on a road to the coastal city of Damascus, he set out to change that and succeeded.

Within just a few generations, this entrepreneurial leader and the other sent ones (or apostles) were said to have turned the world upside down. The flexible organization they established persevered through persecution and hostile attempts from competitors to stamp out their progress. Yet the powerful Roman Empire would crumble even as this venture grew.

New converts responded by the millions to their spiritual message. Local churches, educational institutions, compassionate ministries, and leadership networks would arise and cooperate across geographic borders, crossing racial lines. The poor would be fed, the sick cared for, and the naked clothed. Hospitals, hospices, and orphanages would spring up in cities, towns, and in some of the poorest nations. And Paul's simple but profound letters to his constituents would be read throughout the world and for thousands of years in history's best-seller—the Bible.

AN INCREDIBLE ROLE MODEL

As I read and reread Paul's writings and his story as told by others, I discovered an incredible role model and mentor for leaders. I began to see more clearly the secrets that enabled him to so effectively help launch this movement. His methods of laying new foundations were brilliant—and mostly transferable. I grabbed my pen and a journal and began to write. I asked myself, *Might these insights be helpful to others starting and leading new ventures today?* With my vision sharpened and my soul renewed by the incredible example and teachings of the apostle Paul, I became certain the answer was yes.

My hope is that as you reflect on the principles described in the following chapters you will discover ways to turn your dreams into realities. Hopefully these insights will enable you to avoid needlessly hitting walls and damaging what you most want to protect in your mission. I pray that no matter where you are on your spiritual journey, you will nurture your soul and thrive in all areas of your life.

I hope for you that, like Paul, you will someday complete what you've started and can confidently say, "I have finished the course. I have kept the faith."

1

Desire Something More

The witnesses laid their clothes at the feet of a young man named Saul.

ACTS 7:58

People who knew Saul may have described him as passionate, hardworking, articulate, and highly intelligent—a nearly unbeatable combination of traits. He was the member of a law-abiding, austere sect of Judaism known as the Pharisees. His exemplary lifestyle qualified him to be known as "a Hebrew of Hebrews."

In his performance of religious duty, he was without fault. He spoke his prayers fervently, observed religious feasts, and studied the Jewish law. Even his clothing identified him as a devout Jew. Few would question that this young man was intense, intelligent, and faithful.

These same characteristics probably meant that young Saul wasn't the most pleasant person to be around. Who wants to spend time with someone who is self-righteous, judgmental, and rigid?

From the beginning it seems clear that Saul was determined to be a player. As reflected by his degrees in religion and law and his ascent in political circles at a young age, he refused to be a mere spectator and let life pass him by. His soul wasn't content with the status quo. If he saw a mountain peak, I think he would have climbed it. If he were fighting a war, he would have requested frontline assignments.

As a religious Jew living in the first-century city of Tarsus, Saul's front lines were the religious battles of the day. When a fringe group of people proclaimed that a man called Jesus of Nazareth was the long-awaited Savior of the Jews, Saul couldn't contain himself. He launched into the center of the action in order to squelch what he viewed as blasphemy. Although he only held their coats, Saul stood by and watched as an angry mob stoned to death one of Jesus' followers, a man named Stephen. Then, not satisfied to be a spectator, he rode off to attain permission to arrest other followers as traitors to the state and Judaism.

Though grossly misguided, young Saul was on the hunt for something worthy of his abilities and passions. He had an inner ache that couldn't be satisfied with passive survival. He believed his life was significant, and he was on a quest to prove it. Saul exemplified a quality the entrepreneurial leader can't function without: burning desire.

Saul exemplified a quality the entrepreneurial leader can't function without: burning desire.

In his book *Fast Company*, Keith H. Hammonds writes, "Real entrepreneurs are different from the rest of us. They pursue lives of extremes— extreme ideas and expectations, extreme workloads."[1] Sound familiar?

If you have the entrepreneurial urge in you, your business plan, your capital, your knowledge of consumers, and your great idea are not the most valuable things you have going for you. The single most important quality you can possess is a burning passion that motivates you to seek to turn your dream into a reality—a passion that makes you willing to take the risk and gives you a divine dissatisfaction with the status quo.

Country singer Garth Brooks' song, "The River" describes it this way. He sings of those who are unwilling to "sit upon the shoreline and say [they're] satisfied." Instead they "choose to chance the rapids and dare to dance the tide."[2] In other words, entrepreneurs leave their comfort zones and sign up for the great adventure—they can't *not* go.

This character trait personified Saul of Tarsus. From his youth, he possessed a kind of bullish determination and desire, a need to get involved. "His immense intellectual powers alone would have made him someone to be remembered," said leadership historian J. Oswald Sanders.[3] But Paul's brains could never be matched by his sheer guts. He was a man destined for greatness.

Teddy Roosevelt articulated such entrepreneurial longings when he wrote,

> *The credit belongs to the man in the arena, whose face is marred by dust and sweat and blood, who strives valiantly . . . who knows the great enthusiasm, the great devotions, who spends himself in a worthy cause, who at the best knows in the end the triumph of high achievement, and who at the worst, if he fails, at least fails while daring greatly, so that his place shall never be with those cold and timid souls who have never known neither victory nor defeat.*[4]

Such an adventurous spirit, however, doesn't always produce positive results. Years after his conversion the apostle Paul reflected on his youthful zeal. *I too was convinced that I ought to do all that was possible to oppose the name of Jesus of Nazareth . . . In my obsession against them, I even went to foreign cities to persecute them* (Acts. 26:9-11). Desire and ambition are not always good things. Unbridled and not channeled properly, they can damage or destroy.

Desire can be redeemed to bring about great things in our world: benevolence to millions in need, the discovery and spread of life-saving technology, the creation of new products and jobs, the establishment of new churches to meet the spiritual needs of the hungry in heart. If you read the New Testament, you'll notice God didn't squelch the ambitious part of Saul, forcing him to become a passive milquetoast void of desire. No, transformed by Christ, Paul channeled this intensity, clothed his desire and zeal with love, and unleashed one of the greatest movements of all time—the Christian Church.

Not every idea is worthy of your investment of time and energy.

Not every idea is worthy of your investment of time and energy. Some entrepreneurial ideas are, like Saul's early exploits, self-serving acts, full of "me, myself, and I." They have little regard for others and do much damage along the way. Such entrepreneurs possess a human restlessness that demands its way out in the quest for money, power, or fame, regardless of what it has to do to get there. But we are called to something higher.

Yes, there are days when you will feel driven to prove your worth and to use your gifts to achieve something dramatic. At what cost? Paul demonstrated that there is a better way! There is a way to take that burning desire and work for something that really makes a difference. There is also a way to accomplish it that will produce life in you and benefit others as you utilize your entrepreneurial gifts. It is a way that enables you to care for your soul as the best in you is released. It is not blindly driven, but produces life born out of freedom.

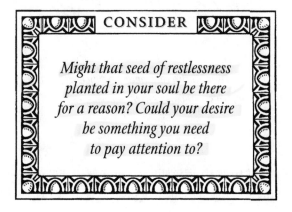

CONSIDER

Might that seed of restlessness planted in your soul be there for a reason? Could your desire be something you need to pay attention to?

2

Getting Knocked Off Your Horse

I fell to the ground and heard a voice say to me,
"Saul! Saul! Why do you persecute me?"

ACTS 22:7

One moment he traveled arrogantly on his way to single-handedly stamp out the growing movement of people claiming Jesus to be their king. The next moment he lay face down in the dust wondering what hit him. A blinding light flashed and a thundering voice from Heaven challenged, *Saul, Saul, why do you persecute me?* Another translation puts it this way, *Why are you kicking against the goads?* In the modern vernacular, "Just who in the world do you think you are!"

Saul-of-Tarsus types have the potential to accomplish much through willpower and self-promotion. Saul could very likely have entered the history books and created a large path of influence by the force of personality and pedigree. "His immense intellectual powers alone would have made him someone to be remembered, even if he had never become a Christian," said scholar and theologian J. Oswald Sanders.[5]

Born in the impressive Mediterranean city of Tarsus, one of the three great university cities of the day (the others being Athens and Alexandria), Saul grew up among an elite group of intellectuals. Invited to train at the feet of the great Jewish scholar Gamaliel, Saul quickly became an expert in religious, legal, and philosophical matters. At the young age of about thirty, it is likely that he sat on the supreme Jewish legal and civil court known as the Sanhedrin. (See Acts 26:10.) Saul was good, and he knew it. He was bent on exploiting his position and gaining opportunity for all it was worth.

Saul was good, and he knew it. He was bent on exploiting his position and gaining opportunity for all it was worth.

It is not a part of many "How to Be a Success" books today, but the Bible clearly states that pride and self-confidence may be helpful for a while—but there exists an even higher way: humility, service, and compassion. In fact we read, *God opposes the proud* (1 Peter 5:5). He stands in the face of those who believe "It's all about me."

With value in the opposite, God *gives grace to the humble* (1 Peter 5:5). The Bible cautions arrogant entrepreneurs with the words, *Now listen, you who say, "Today or tomorrow we will go to this or that city, spend a year there, carry on business and make money. Instead you ought to say, "If it is the Lord's will, we will live and do this or that"* (James 4:13, 15). Jesus' teaching is clear, *Whoever wants to become great among you must be your servant* (Matthew 20:26). *Everyone who exalts himself will be humbled, and he who humbles himself will be exalted* (Luke 18:14).

That doesn't mean the entrepreneurial "get it going" gift isn't worthwhile or that all ambition is wrong. The issue is one of the heart—"Why do we want to do this?" *Humble yourselves, therefore, under God's mighty hand, that he may lift you up in due time* (1 Peter 5:6). Saul of Tarsus did not heed this advice. He sped full steam ahead, bent on his self-proclaimed mission to eradicate all the followers of the Way of Jesus. *I even obtained letters from them to their brothers in Damascus, and went there to bring these people as prisoners to Jerusalem to be punished* (Acts 22:5), he recounts.

God's reaction to Saul's pride was a direct ambush—blinding lights from heaven flashing; a thunderous voice from heaven; and the question, the stunning question, *Saul! Saul! Why do you persecute me?* By this time, Saul was on the ground, blinded, stuttering, and frazzled by this direct encounter with God. The independent, self-reliant Saul of Tarsus found himself in the dust, unable to see. We read that he *could see nothing* (Acts 9:8). Others led him to Damascus; He must have found this very humbling. The beginning of Saul's basic training, lesson number one, "Don't forget God is God. You are not!"

"Ego is a deadly killer in organizations, businesses, churches, and entrepreneurial enterprises," teaches author and consultant Ken Blanchard. It wreaks havoc on the soul of a person and the soul of an organization. "I call it—Edging God Out—EGO," says Blanchard. "It arrogantly proclaims, 'I am all powerful . . . I am God.' There is a better way. A different kind of leadership."[6]

"Ego is a deadly killer in organizations, businesses, churches, and entrepreneurial enterprises."

Saul wouldn't have signed up for the cutting edge of personal growth in leadership training. It wasn't honorable or something to put on a résumé. Instead it was quite humbling—a divine swat. Paul experienced the opportunity to be knocked off his horse of self-reliance and blind ambition, and received an invitation to submit to the bigger plan designed by the Almighty himself. It was a humble submission to another agenda, a call to move from striving to achieve for self to following after a call, from self-accomplishment to a mission for the good of humanity, from ambition to prove one's significance to a humble sense of being motivated by love. It was a move from "It's all about me" to a humble desire to make a difference for others.

For some of us, this journey is a gradual and gentle process. With time, we recognize the importance of investing our lives in what will truly outlast us. We get the picture that it really is better to serve than to be served or to give than to receive. If that's you, consider yourself blessed.

Some of us may need to be beat up a little before we will listen. We've grown accustomed to doing it "my way." We've learned to ring a bell and expect service. We personify the country song, "Lord It's Hard to Be Humble": "Well, just look at me, will ya?" *Until*—the day comes when we fall off a horse or two. We lose a job. Our company teeters. A loved one walks out. Horses we perceived as stable and sure-footed throw us. Dazed, we wonder, *What's wrong with this animal? Why this pain? Why this dust in my mouth? Who turned out the lights? Who messed up things here? Where are You, God?*

It is at this point that we, like Saul, have a choice. We can either suck it up and try to move on our own agenda—maybe faster, harder, and tougher; or we can surrender our egos. We can submit to God. We can say, "God, here I am. I'll do whatever You want. I'll follow You and get off this horse."

It took a dramatic encounter on the road to Damascus, but Saul finally surrendered. It revealed a new future, changing his life and the course of history forever.

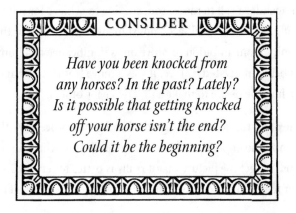

CONSIDER

Have you been knocked from any horses? In the past? Lately? Is it possible that getting knocked off your horse isn't the end? Could it be the beginning?

3

Know Your Calling

Paul, called to be an apostle of Christ Jesus by the will of God.

1 CORINTHIANS 1:1

Consider this FAQ (Frequently Asked Question): "What am I supposed to do with my life?" Paul learned the answer to that question after the dramatic events on the road to Damascus: *This man is my chosen instrument to carry my name before the Gentiles and their kings and before the people of Israel* (Acts 9:15).

What Paul was called to do and who he was were one and the same—inseparable. *Paul, called to be an apostle of Christ Jesus by the will of God.* It wasn't because Paul earned a degree, inherited the family business, or chose the most lucrative course. No, this *was* Paul. It was an expression of who God intended him to be, and he knew it.

So what about those of us who haven't had such a divine encounter, yet are equipped with gifts and a burning desire to create, establish, invent, oversee, teach, or write? What if we have no clear direction?

The fourth-century church father Eusebius asserted a philosophy that is widely held today. He described the perfect life and the permitted life. He held that the perfect life is that of those who give themselves fully to prayer, contemplation, the priesthood, or a benevolence ministry. The permitted life belongs to those with secular jobs: craftsmen, soldiers, traders, government leaders, farmers, and mothers. As historian and philosopher, Os Guiness put it, those living the "permitted life have a kind of secondary grade of piety."[7]

Many today, however, are discovering that one may be called to professions other than the ministry. My friend Matt discovered after several years of service as an assistant pastor that his calling wasn't to preach sermons. It is to write computer code! He says, "When I write code, I feel the smile of God! I didn't feel that way when I worked at the church." Martin Luther said it well, "The works of monks and priests, however holy and arduous they be, do not differ one whit in the sight of God from the works of the rustic laborers in the field or the woman going about her household tasks."[8]

Those who discover their God-given callings tap into a dynamic direction and confidence that can only come from the Creator himself. Life takes on new purpose and is charged with a sense of rightness that goes way beyond any vain desire for glory or success. It frees these individuals to fully become who God created them to be, fully alive and energized in all they do.

Those who discover their God-given callings
tap into a dynamic direction and confidence
that can only come from the Creator himself.

For too long, many have been satisfied to get a job or make a living, with financial success the primary goal. In so doing many have tried to be people they aren't, and it doesn't work. They have felt empty, frustrated, and out of place. If this describes you, it may be time to take a different course of action and do what you do best. In fact, it may feel too easy and not like work at all, but it's what you were meant to do and who you were meant to be.

In his book *Let Your Life Speak,* Parker Palmer advises, "Before you tell your life what you intend to do with it, listen for what it intends to do with you." Palmer continues, "The deepest vocational question is not 'What ought I to do with my life?' It is more elemental and demanding . . . 'Who am I?' 'What is my nature?'"[9] Furthermore, Frederick Buechner asserts that your calling is "the place where your deepest gladness meets the world's deep need." In other words, it's your zone.

You may not receive your purpose as a once-and-for-all "Do this" or "Go there." However, there are many clues to help you discover it. Look at your personality. What are you good at? What do the people who know you best say about you? What tasks bring you a deep and satisfying pleasure? What do you do that bears good fruit in the lives of others? What is your dream? What makes you feel most alive?

For Paul this meant reaching the Gentiles with the message of the Gospel, establishing new churches, instructing them, and finding new leaders to mentor. Paul said he was compelled (Acts 20:22). He couldn't refuse his work. His work caused him to stay true to who he was. Like Paul, you may already know your purpose. Your dream is crystal clear; it compels you. In that, persevere. Don't shrink back. Follow the call.

For others of us, things haven't been quite so clear. We haven't known that we could approach things with purpose. We just did things because others thought we should, because they were lucrative, or because there were job openings. We may feel stuck—stuck having to be something we aren't, day in and day out. What a waste to do things we were never cut out to do. We feel continuously drained of life energy and wonder if we will forever feel this way.

You have the opportunity to fully express your calling, to manage your own career. You can discover your deepest passion and do what unleashes your greatest surge of energy. Like the title of a book by William Bridges, you can create *You and Company.* In this same book, James Russell Lowell makes a profound statement: "No one is born into the world whose work is not born with him."[10] You can choose a profession that reflects who you really are, rather than living as the definition of what you do.

> You can discover your deepest passion and do what unleashes your greatest surge of energy.

As an entrepreneur, you likely receive great satisfaction from creating something new, setting new processes in motion, or seeing people benefit from your labor. You are dissatisfied with the status quo and see unmet needs and untapped potential. You have a burning desire to do something different—chart a new course or pioneer a new technology. You realize what isn't being done and are obsessed with the thought, *Why isn't someone doing that?* Well, that *someone* may be you!

Paul engaged his calling, and today the world is a different place. What might happen if you were to engage yours? What would be the cost?

Your purpose need not be as enormous in scope as Paul's, but it does have to be a reflection of *you!* You must lean into what and who you really are, leave behind the safe shores of stereotypical success, and chart the path God has given you. The risks are completely worthwhile because this is what you were created for.

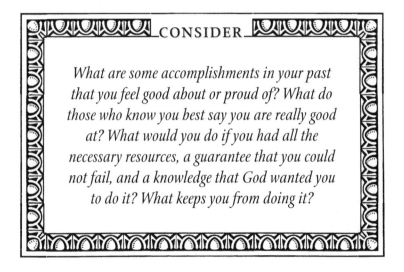

CONSIDER

What are some accomplishments in your past that you feel good about or proud of? What do those who know you best say you are really good at? What would you do if you had all the necessary resources, a guarantee that you could not fail, and a knowledge that God wanted you to do it? What keeps you from doing it?

4

Grow in the Desert

Nor did I go up to Jerusalem to see those who were apostles before I was, but I went immediately into Arabia.

GALATIANS 1:17

Paul headed for the Arabian Desert prior to engaging in his life's work. The go-getter, the activist, became a recluse instead of sprinting to preach his message. Wisely, he recognized the needs of his own soul—preparation, consecration, healing—and he enrolled in the spiritual boot camp for the soul. The desert did exactly what deserts can do—if we let them.

Deserts, figuratively or literally, present special challenges to those of us who like to control our environment and keep things comfortable. "The immensity of the desert overwhelms both the power and weakness of men," wrote Ivan Illich.[11] Deserts aren't known for fun, convenience, or pleasure. Simple survival takes work; stamina is tested. Deserts are dry, dusty, brittle, and barren—endless and devastatingly lonely. Surroundings are often hostile, even dangerous. It takes great exertion to accomplish anything.

Deserts, figuratively or literally, present special
challenges to those of us who like to control our
environment and keep things comfortable.

So why go there? The desert can tame the soul, if we will let it. It can
shape a human doing back into a human being. We must realize we
can't control everything. When we give up the belief that we're simply
the accumulation of our productivity, priorities change. There is little
use for all the toys and money we've labored to amass. Our jobs no
longer define us. If we let it, the desert can strip away our pride and
self-centeredness. We can develop thick skin and a tender heart. We
realize it's okay to need others and that we can survive on very little.
Most importantly, we learn that we can depend on God; and since He
is in control, we don't have to be.

Most entrepreneurial leaders visit the desert at one time or another.
There are many biblical examples, such as Moses who fled to the
desert after killing an Egyptian. While in the desert, God spoke to him
through a burning bush. David, the great king of Israel, fled to the
desert to escape death by the jealous King Saul. While there, he wrote
one of the many beloved psalms of the Bible: *My soul thirsts for you
[God] . . . in a dry and weary land where there is no water* (Psalm 63:1).
Prophets often emerged from times in the desert. Jesus himself went to
the desert for forty days and forty nights, enduring agonizing tempta-
tion before he launched His public ministry.

Other historical examples abound of the inner leader cultivated through
times in the desert. Abraham Lincoln, a simple rail-splitter, spent much
time in his desert. He lost his first love before they could be married, and

he then lost one election after another. Finally, however, he emerged as the leader of our nation. Yet while there, he endured more pain over the tragic death of his son Willie. Many attribute Lincoln's great strength under pressure to his ability to experience loss and endure.

Historians view Franklin Roosevelt's bout with polio as the very thing that made him compassionate toward others in pain. Against the enormous pressure of German bombardments, Winston Churchill boldly held out, "My whole life has been a preparation for this." Juan Trippe, the visionary creator of the Boeing 747 believed he could design a plane that would keep his company from bankruptcy.

In his book, *Letters from the Desert*, Catholic writer and desert monastic Carlo Corretto shares why he moved to the desert. He wrote,

> *The Lord conducted me into the real desert because I was so thick-skinned. For me, it was necessary. But all that sand was not enough to erase the dirt from my soul . . . . But the same way is not for everybody. And if you cannot go into the desert, you must nonetheless 'make some desert' in your life. Every now and then leaving men and looking for solitude to restore, in prolonged silence and prayer, the stuff of your soul . . . . But the desert is not the final stopping place. It is a stage on the journey . . . . Our vocation is contemplation in the streets."[12]*

Desert seasons are often slow and unproductive. We can experience weeks, months, or even years in our desert, asking ourselves, "Where did I go wrong? Why is this so hard?" We can feel isolated, lonely, and abandoned. We wonder if we'll ever get out of this God-forsaken rut! Deserts are just plain hard.

Ultimately, deserts teach us the power of simplicity. We're reminded that everything does not revolve around us—that the responsibility for changing the world is not on our shoulders. There is Someone who still opens and closes doors from above. When we slow down long enough, we can see that *Man does not live on bread alone* (Matthew 4:4). We learn that our worth is not based on what we do, but we are worth infinitely more than what we could ever accomplish. We are loved, period. Life is a gift; enjoy it!

Ultimately, deserts teach us the power of simplicity. We're reminded that everything does not revolve around us—that the responsibility for changing the world is not on our shoulders.

Sometimes the desert is less obvious, and we simply feel frustrated. We exert, try, hustle, and struggle—but with little result. Most noticeably, we can't seem to accomplish all we'd like. Our lists and goals go unchecked, and we feel held back. Though much can be happening on the inside, we don't see tangible results on the outside. If we yield, however, we become less dependent upon our circumstances to be happy; we break free of the need for black-and-white solutions and quick fixes.

I hate deserts too! I sometimes refer to one of mine as "the decade between 1992 and 1995." I was terminally confused! After years of seeming success and outer accolades, everything seemed to disintegrate. The leadership team I recruited to start a church in Boston walked away frustrated and disgruntled. The grants never materialized, and the bank account dwindled. Daily I fought the voices within me that said, "I told you so!" and "This is impossible." I couldn't get anything to work the way I wanted it to—including my own inner tinkering. I couldn't rely on my degrees or my hard work. Although I knew I needed to be patient, I wasn't.

Paul didn't avoid his desert. He faced it head on and emerged a better leader and a better man. He didn't want to learn second hand. He embraced his desert and did not avoid the pain, the darkness, or the solitude. It is at this point that the mocking voices fade. The drive slacks off. The intensity is replaced by simple faith—if we let it.

As you allow your deserts to shape you, you will unlock and discover a new ability to bear lasting fruit, and then, like Paul, you will develop the ability to endure the ups and downs of life with confidence and hope.

Of course, the choice is up to you.

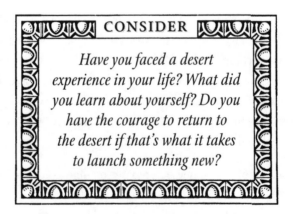

CONSIDER

Have you faced a desert experience in your life? What did you learn about yourself? Do you have the courage to return to the desert if that's what it takes to launch something new?

5

Seek Mentors

*After three years, I went up to Jerusalem to get acquainted
with Peter and stayed with him fifteen days.*

GALATIANS 1:18

Leaders today hunger for mentors, those who will come alongside and
share their journey and what they have learned. Mentors act as guides.
They don't necessarily share what they would do in your shoes, but
they help you discover what *you* need to do. It is said that the average
person accomplishes only 10 percent of his or her potential. It's
obvious that we need more mentors.

Webster's dictionary defines the term *mentor* as "a wise and faithful
advisor, a tutor." Mentors were present in many ancient stories. In
Homer's *Odyssey,* for example, Odysseus is asked to watch over the
development of his son, Telemachus. More recent examples are the
mentors depicted in the *Star Wars* trilogy.

Those on a journey often look for wise guidance from others who have
traveled that road. Explorers Lewis and Clark recruited Native American
guides as they explored the West. Mount Everest climbers hire the native
Sherpas to guide them up the perilous slopes. As we set out to explore
our own distant lands, we seek those who are willing to share what

they've already learned and who will take the time to ask, "How's it going?" We need them to listen to what we have to say—the good and the bad, our discoveries and deep questions. As author Eugene Peterson said, we seek "people to be encountered, not just observed."[13]

From the start, Paul sought mentors. Although he had a wellspring of intellectual knowledge and training in the Scripture as a Pharisee, he journeyed to Jerusalem to meet Peter and *stayed with him fifteen days* (Galatians 1:18). You can imagine the rich discussions during those two weeks. Most likely, Paul inquired about Peter's experience during his three-year relationship with Jesus, his life as an apostle, and about the ways the Church functioned. I imagine they talked about what worked and what didn't in spreading the Message. Certainly, Paul shared his conversion experience with Peter.

Paul wisely surrounded himself with seasoned leaders like Barnabus and then Priscilla and Aquilla, a husband and wife team who Paul said, *risked their lives for me* (Romans 16:3). Before he launched out on his own mission, he was recorded to have lived among the other leaders and prophets in Antioch (Acts 13:1).

The wise writer of Proverbs wrote, *Make plans by seeking advice; if you wage war, obtain guidance* (Proverbs 20:18). In other words, seek counsel; get outside input. I emphasize the word *outside* because those closest to you may have difficulty in being objective. They may not want to tell you the truth. They may have stakes in the outcome.

The wise writer of Proverbs wrote,
Make plans by seeking advice; if you wage war, obtain guidance (Proverbs 20:18).

So where are the mentors today? Where are those older men and women who will offer guidance, perspective, and themselves? How can you recognize a mentor? I asked these same questions myself. I also whined, "There aren't any mentors out there. I'm out here on my own! Why doesn't anyone want to mentor me?"

Finally, my wife Mindy asked me, "Jeff, have you ever prayed for a mentor or asked anyone to mentor you?"

I responded, "Well, um. . . not really. But, I'll try it," I told her, only half-believing my prayer would be answered.

Three weeks later I found myself sitting across the table from Bruce, an experienced entrepreneurial leader, author, and consultant. It was as if the lights went on. He didn't have *mentor* written across his forehead; but it was clear. "Bruce," I nervously asked, "This may seem like a strange question, but would you be open to continue meeting together? Maybe in kind of a mentoring relationship? I'm learning so much by being with you. I'd love to continue this relationship"

He thought for a moment. I held my breath. "Jeff," he said, "I'd be honored."

Almost six years later, Bruce is still a very close friend and mentor, meeting with me every couple of months and talking on the phone about every two weeks. After that initial visit with Bruce, I began to meet regularly with another man, Jim, as a spiritual mentor. A gym teacher by trade, Jim met with me every few weeks to talk about spiritual issues, parenting, and entrepreneurial ministry. I feel incredibly indebted to both of these men, and Mindy does too!

Most mentors don't just come to us, and you usually won't stumble upon them. They're sought out. We need to be willing to meet with these individuals and simply ask. Mentors come in all ages with varied occupations. Some mentors today have made a career as personal or executive coaches because they enjoy helping others succeed. Just as top athletes benefit enormously from the work of a coach, ordinary people can benefit from the work of a mentor.

Most mentors don't just come to us, and you usually won't stumble upon them. They're sought out.

When you meet personally or by phone, there's no need to follow a formal curriculum or program. Share what's going on in your life and in your endeavors. Talk honestly about your struggles, obstacles, and breakthroughs—and then *listen.*

It is essential to find a safe place to process the things that are discussed. "Counseling has become a profession," says psychologist Larry Crabb "not just because of the expertise but because of the safety . . . . Psychotherapists know one thing. When you're hurting it helps to talk with someone you trust."[14] The best mentors and coaches facilitate just that—a safe place to process. The purpose is not to ascertain what the mentor would do, but to help you discover what you could do, what is right for you.

Chemistry is important too. "Coaching can work magically . . . if the chemistry is right," said a business professor at the University of California.[15] Seek out someone whom you feel drawn to, and interview the individual. Do you feel safe with this person? Do you respect him or her? If so, prioritize the time together. Share what's really going on and listen to what he or she shares.

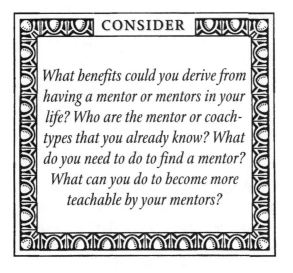

CONSIDER

What benefits could you derive from having a mentor or mentors in your life? Who are the mentor or coach-types that you already know? What do you need to do to find a mentor? What can you do to become more teachable by your mentors?

6

Be Sent

They placed their hands on them and sent them off.

ACTS 13:3

The call to entrepreneurial leadership takes us from the safety of what already exists to the unknown territory where we establish something new. It involves laying new foundations where no one else has built, going where others would never dream of going. This will sometimes bring us into hostile and foreign places. At other times, it simply introduces change to the status quo. It could be in a place or an organization. Maybe it is a jumbled project that appears stuck or lifeless. Whatever the case, it usually involves risk. We will need to persevere; there may be a high price to pay.

If that's not enough, many will *not* go with you. There may be times when you will feel alone and misunderstood—often by the very people you want to help or those you wished would be your allies. They may question your sanity. "Are you sure you're doing the right thing?" Soon you, too, may question if you're doing the right thing and are on track!

You will need a home base—a support group—those who know what you are doing and care. They believe in you and your vision, and they're behind you. They know you and care that you succeed. They care that you are healthy and whole—spiritually, emotionally, and physically. They ask you how you *really* are and actually listen.

Its been said that everyone would be wise to have a personal board of directors, or, as my friend Dave calls them, a board for life. They are more than a board that oversees your work or endeavor; they help you steward your life. They act as a sounding board, a mirror, and they give you a healthy dose of reality. Entrepreneurial leaders need such people almost more than anyone else as they enter uncharted territories.

> Its been said that everyone would be wise to have a personal board of directors. They are more than a board that oversees your work or endeavor; they help you steward your life.

This board is a group of people who love you deeply but are not afraid of you. They tell you the truth. They are willing to say the hard things. Yet, they will not seek to quench your dreams and bind you to status quos. They provide a safe place to share ideas, opportunities, and possibilities; a place to share the good and the bad, and the confusions as well as the disappointments and downturns. They are your safe place; they are real friends.

A few months ago, I asked a man who once served as the president and CEO of a major technology corporation in the Northeast what his greatest challenges had been. "Very sadly," he said, "I didn't have anyone I could really share with. I felt alone. I wish I could have changed that."

Paul had that group of people from the start. The leaders of the church of Antioch affirmed his call (along with that of his partner Barnabus) as valid and from God. They released him to embrace his call. They stood behind him and laid hands on him as a symbol of their solidarity. Then, after a time away, Paul returned to his sending post and gave them an update. We read, *They gathered the church together and reported all that God had done through them and how he had opened the door of faith to the Gentiles. And they stayed there a long time with the disciples* (Acts 14:27-28).

That must have been quite a homecoming. They cared about what they were doing when the vast majority of those they encountered on the field did not. They most likely shared the highs and the lows; the successes and the setbacks.

If you have not yet launched your entrepreneurial venture, begin to develop such a home base. You might even go to those you trust and who know you well, and seek their blessing on what you are about to embark upon. This is especially important if you are about to undertake a spiritual endeavor. Share your dream, the vision of the future. Ask them to provide accountability, to be a mirror to reflect back to you as you proceed. Encourage them to ask the tough questions. Invite them to help you keep your priorities straight, whatever comes your way. Ask them to investigate the way you care for your soul, your family, and your physical fitness.

Just a note of caution: some who are not called to be entrepreneurial leaders may not understand your vision or your call and may consider it dangerous, overly ambitious, or frivolous. Listen to them, but be discerning. Are their fears founded or not? If they are not entrepreneurs themselves, they may not be able to imagine how someone could do what you want to do! They may not be your best advisors. You may want to seek out other entrepreneurial leaders for their feedback.

The other extreme is to start something without support or being sent. Some ignore the warnings of their advisors. Today I received news of another "just do it" entrepreneur who is floundering after three years of confusion, discouragement, and setbacks. His vision to start base camps all over the country for extreme risk sports was bold and exciting. He envisioned camps in Colorado, North Carolina, Montana, and Florida. He set out to raise millions of dollars in capital and to recruit key people to his organization. He had a big vision, but he admitted he had little patience initially to build a support team before launching out. "It just has taken so much longer than I thought it would."

No amount of support or sending can smooth the path entirely or assure success, but it can't hurt! You might gain vital information that will spare you a lot of pain, and the very ones who send you now may provide invaluable support in the future.

No amount of support or sending can smooth the path entirely or assure success, but it can't hurt!

Sometimes we need to listen to the voice of wisdom that says, "Don't do something just to be doing something. Sit there. Be patient." Share the vision and the dream, but wait until those around you affirm you, send you, stand with you and behind you. Then with that, *go!* Be an agent of change and live out your call.

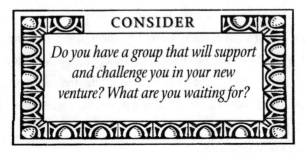

CONSIDER

Do you have a group that will support and challenge you in your new venture? What are you waiting for?

7

Meet Real Needs

We know that if the earthly tent we live in is destroyed,
we have a building from God, an eternal house in heaven.

2 CORINTHIANS 5:1

Saint Paul realized that his call was to meet a spiritual need. People searched for meaning in life. They looked for a reason to have hope for the future. Paul was in direct sales. His market was comprised of those whose *earthly tents* (bodies) would be *destroyed* (through death). He communicated what could meet their needs—Heaven. He told his audience how to get there, what it was all about.

Paul was a man compelled. He described it this way: *Woe to me if I do not preach* (1 Corinthians 9:16). He couldn't *not* meet the spiritual needs of those around him. His paycheck couldn't be measured in dollars and cents, but in the sense of fulfillment, which was priceless to him. He knew he was accomplishing his mission; he was meeting a need. He didn't need a paycheck to motivate him; the call compelled him forward, enabled him to rise above difficult circumstances. He was *hard pressed on every side, but not crushed; perplexed, but not in despair* (2 Corinthians 4:8).

As mentioned earlier, Frederick Buechner wrote, "Calling is where your deepest joy and the world's needs meet."[16] Sometimes it makes you cry. Other times it makes you so excited that you can't sit still. You turn red. You pound your fist. You can't help it. As Emerson put it, less emotionally, you just long to "leave the world a bit better."[17]

Today, more of us seek purpose beyond our paychecks. We've tried success defined as more, bigger, or better. It left us empty. We want to find satisfaction not only for a job well done, but also for a job done with a greater purpose. Meeting real needs while staying true to whom God made us to be—*that* is success!

Meeting real needs while staying true to whom God made us to be—*that* is success!

Over coffee, I asked a man who started his own successful financial-planning business what advice he would give someone else starting out in business. He thought for a second, then said, "Focus on the number of people you're impacting—not the financial success. That's made all the difference for me." He continued, "I have helped hundreds of people find financial freedom."

A young but seasoned entrepreneur whom I coach told me, "I feel so dirty about some of the things I've done. I'm ready to make sure my heart is pure in the things I do in the future." A clear conscience is vital to experiencing true fulfillment.

Tom Chappell, founder of Tom's of Maine said something similar:

Something in us wants to endure beyond retained earnings, and that something is our soul . . . . At Tom's of Maine, doing good is at the center of the business enterprise. Doing good is, in fact, the reason we're doing well . . . . Setting out to be the lowest-cost pro- ducer is meaningful only if you also set out to be the highest quality giver; today's discerning consumers demand both.[18]

Entrepreneurial leaders have an opportunity to set strategies, processes, and organizations into motion that can meet genuine needs. They can do an enormous amount of good in the world. They have the potential to create invaluable products, services, agencies, or systems to make our world a better place to live. They create publications, educational material, and spread information. They provide food, clothing, shelter, and leisure. They fulfill the need for new technologies, life-saving devices, investment ideas, and ministries to help hurting people. The needs in our world are enormous. The entrepreneurial leader has an opportunity to meet those needs. As Tom Chappell said, "You don't have to sell your soul to make your numbers. . . . Suddenly I found a way to manage for profit and for the common good."[19]

"Others think we're nuts," said an entrepreneur presently working out of a friend's garage, creating medical devices to assist stroke victims. "They'd never do what we're doing, but strokes are the third leading cause of death. I feel like we've got something here! I want to use my skills and knowledge to do something about that." He went on to say, "Some entrepreneurs are motivated by financial gain, others by glory. . . . Those have some interest to me, but most of all, I'm interested in meeting the need. I feel compelled by it."

This meeting of needs doesn't mean that entrepreneurial leaders shouldn't receive recognition for taking the risk or reward with a reasonable profit. I've heard it said, "We don't live to breathe, but we do live by breathing." In the same way, we don't work for profits, but we can't work without them." Meaningful work involves much more than profits. If there are no good reasons in our minds to do what we're doing, we may need to reassess. Why not explore doing the very thing that we would do, even if we weren't paid to do it. It might result in a winning situation all the way around!

Why not explore doing the very thing that we would do, even if we weren't paid to do it.

What are the needs that you feel compelled to meet? What gets your blood flowing and makes you bang your fist on the table? Do you, your product, or your idea meet a real need? Can you articulate it in one word or in a sentence? Think to yourself, *If this entrepreneurial endeavor doesn't succeed, what would our world be without?*

Then realize that you might be God's hands and feet to meet this need on the earth. You and your organization may be the answer to that problem. You may be the ones who create the joy for a child? You may create a way to feed homeless people or create a community for the lonely? When all is said and done, your legacy will live on, in and through the many lives you've touched.

Meet real needs.

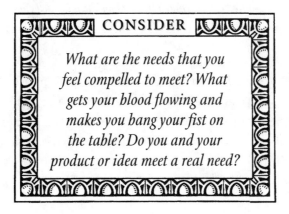

CONSIDER

What are the needs that you feel compelled to meet? What gets your blood flowing and makes you bang your fist on the table? Do you and your product or idea meet a real need?

8

Let Go of What You're Not

By the grace God has given me, I laid a foundation as
an expert builder, and someone else is building on it.

1 CORINTHIANS 3:10

In Saint Paul we discover a capable and extremely gifted man. Paul willfully let go of what he was not. He knew where he was proficient: *I laid a foundation as an expert builder.* He also knew his limitations, areas where others were more proficient. *Someone else is building on it.*

Paul knew he was called to establish churches, but he understood where his call ended and where the call of others began. He didn't stay around to lead the churches he established. Paul and his partner Barnabus *appointed elders [church leaders] for them in each church* (Acts 14:23). They entrusted their fledgling flocks to care for and instill leadership in others.

Clearly Paul was gifted in many areas. He could teach, preach, debate, organize, write, and serve as a conduit for healing. Although he received his call in a dramatic manner, he realized it didn't mean he was called to be a one-man show. Unlike some domineering leaders, Paul never sought the limelight. He saw himself as a servant. He knew who he was and what he was uniquely called to be: an *ambassador*

(Ephesians 6:20) of God's message to the Gentiles. Once he completed his assignment, he gladly handed the work to those called to take the church to the next level. Paul let go of what he was not.

Part of our role as entrepreneurial leaders involves continually moving toward doing what we are uniquely created to do. Nineteenth-century evangelist D. L. Moody said, "Give me a man who says this one thing I do, not these fifty I dabble in."[20] This doesn't mean there won't be seasons when we must multi-task in order to accomplish our mission, but if we are tempted to do more and more ourselves, it may be time to simplify. Wait until someone else is brought forth to take over and then delegate. We do our thing; others do theirs.

The challenge for many of us is to quit trying to perfect areas that aren't our strengths. One entrepreneurial leader who leads two companies said he realized he had to take his nose out of the employee's job. "I hired a gifted man to run one of the companies," he told me. "Then I kept telling him what to do. I think I drove the guy nuts! After he left, I realized I had become a bottleneck to the company. Even though he was good at what he did, I just couldn't give up control."

The challenge for many of us is to quit trying to perfect areas that aren't our strengths.

Paul taught the spiritual principle that weaknesses aren't always as counter-productive as they seem. They teach us that we're part of a greater plan. We realize that God is God, and we aren't. Often our most significant work transpires despite our weaknesses. In the midst of his own painful struggle, Paul said that God reminded him: *My grace is sufficient for you, for my power is made perfect in weakness* (2 Corinthians 12:9). He goes on to say, *Therefore I will boast all the more gladly about my weaknesses, so that Christ's power may rest on me.* He acknowledged, *When I am weak, then I am strong* (v. 10). As he let go of what he wasn't, God compensated.

I take my coaching clients through an exercise which asks them to think about their own genius. "What are three things you do really well?" I ask. "What are the things you actually enjoy doing and want to keep doing?" I then write those on the left side of a piece of paper.

Then I ask them to think of three areas of their work they could gladly release to someone who could do the tasks as well, if not better than they would. I then write those on the right side of the paper. Then I ask them, "What does this reveal to you?"

Often they respond, "I need to be willing to give up control of those things on the right, so I can give more time and energy to the things on the left."

After going through this exercise with a man in his twenties, we quickly realized that in his entrepreneurial role, he spent at least 80 percent of his time and an inordinate amount of energy on the non-genius side of the equation. We reviewed these things:

1)   recruiting people to a vision,

2)   administration—organizing lists, projects, etc.,

3)   managing other people's work.

And guess how he felt about his work? He hated it. He continually felt drained. "I think about quitting almost every single day," he admitted.

His areas of genius were: coming up with new ways to do things, writing, and counseling individuals on a one-on-one basis. His areas of weakness took 80 percent of his time and most of his energy, which left him without reserves to do the things he enjoyed.

A few months later, he made a dramatic decision. He courageously turned his work over to someone else and went to work in a larger organization where he could focus on his specialties. I recently received an e-mail from him telling me how much he loves his new life. He shared that he now spends the majority of his time writing new material for youth, guiding them as a mentor, and getting an education. He described his work now with words like *great*, *fun*, and *freeing*. He no longer feels the angst of trying to be what he's not.

Like Paul, you too can move toward spending the vast majority of your time focused on your areas of strength, your calling. The plan is for you to do the things you do best, and let others do theirs. Although the results may not be immediate, over time you will gain more and more energy to accomplish your calling with excellence. A good plan is to set a goal to operate in your areas of strength 90 percent of your time.

The plan is for you to do the things you
do best, and let others do theirs.

Then, begin to let others take over in the areas where you lack strength. Share what you know and give them space. Let graphic artists design. Hire bookkeepers to manage the finances. Bring in others to do the marketing. Whatever the areas are, choose to pursue excellence by letting go of who and what you're not.

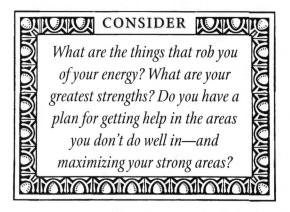

CONSIDER

What are the things that rob you of your energy? What are your greatest strengths? Do you have a plan for getting help in the areas you don't do well in—and maximizing your strong areas?

9

Start

At once he began to preach in the synagogues
that Jesus is the Son of God.

ACTS 9:20

There are plenty of people with great ideas, but few who take their dream and turn it into reality. The willingness to begin makes the difference. "Whatever you do, or dream you can do, begin it. Boldness has genius power, and magic in it," said Johann von Goethe.

Yes, there is a time for analysis and a time for planning. There is a time to be patient, but the time comes to just give it a shot. Even Jesus encouraged risk-taking. *The kingdom of heaven suffers violence,* He said, *and violent men take it by force* (Matthew 11:12 NASB). The tone certainly doesn't advocate passivity.

My friend Vance is an initiator. He's a remarkable entrepreneur who pioneered Goldmine Software into an enormous success. Most recently, he and Steve Smith co-founded a not-for-profit organization called the Foundation of the Heart, and now he hosts transformational retreats for business leaders on a regular basis.

As I continue to get to know Vance, I am impressed by his willingness to move forward. He sees an opportunity and says, "Let's explore that." Vance learned of a meeting in New York, and he made plans to attend.

It's as if Vance has a sixth sense for opportunities where his mission intersects with the world around him. When that happens, he acts. Frankly, others are drawn to his leadership. In less than a year, his non-profit organization attracted numerous staff and volunteers who have moved to Colorado Springs to join his team.

As Albert Schweitzer said, "Example is not the main thing in influencing others. It is the only thing."[21] William Wallace, whose life was chronicled in the hit movie *Braveheart,* motivated his countrymen to rise up against the English who desired to crush Scotland: "Sons of Scotland . . . you have come to fight as free men, and free men you are." Wallace then challenged them to begin . . . even at the risk of their own lives. With his painted blue face and Scottish brogue, he shouts, "And dying in your beds, many years from now, would you be willing to trade all the days from this day to that to come back here and tell our enemies that they may take our lives, but they'll never take our freedom!"[22]

In Ecclesiastes the Bible also calls for action. *Whatever your hand finds to do, do it with all your might* (Ecclesiastes 9:10). In today's vernacular: "Don't just sit there! *Go for it!*" In the same verse, we learn the motivation for such action: *For in the grave, where you are going, there is neither working nor planning nor knowledge nor wisdom.* In other words, when you're dead, you're dead. Like the words of an Olympic speed skater I heard speak a few years ago, "Don't die wondering."[23] William Wallace may have stated it best in his classic words, "Every man dies, but not every man truly lives."[24]

"Don't just sit there! *Go for it!*"

It takes wisdom to discern whether it is time to act or whether you are just being impatient. Once the time to launch finally arrives, it usually brings a feeling of relief. It's time to get things rolling.

Author John Ortberg titled his book about faith, *If You Want to Walk on the Water, You'll Have to Get out of the Boat.*[25] The title itself is compelling and is a truth that all entrepreneurial leaders can relate to. Can't you just imagine Jesus inviting modern-day Peters to walk into areas where there is no solid ground and they have no choice but to trust? They've never walked on water, and it appears ridiculously impossible. In the biblical account, Peter wants reassurance. *Lord, if it's you,* he says, *tell me to come to you on the water.* Jesus replied, *"Come"* (Matthew 14:28-29).

There certainly are good reasons not to jump into risky entrepreneurial waters, but fear of failure should not be among them. Fear has been defined as "False Evidence Appearing Real." You will need to do some serious soul searching. Are you dealing with fear, or do you just need more faith? Are you afraid of failure, or is the venture truly impossible? Are you afraid to look foolish or in need of wise counsel? Are you fearful of losing money, or do you need to be more conservative in your spending? Ask yourself what opportunity you would miss if you never started this thing. How would this affect you, others, and the world?

> There certainly are good reasons not to jump into risky entrepreneurial waters, but fear of failure should not be among them.

Saint Paul was a bold starter. He seized the day and its opportunities. In Pisidian Antioch, a general invitation went forward, *Brothers, if you have a message of encouragement for the people, please speak* (Acts 13:15). The very next sentence reveals the one person to act: *Standing up, Paul motioned with his hand and said, "Men of Israel and you Gentiles who worship God, listen to me!"* (v. 16).

Acts 16:10 provides another example of Paul in action. *After Paul had seen the vision, we got ready at once to leave for Macedonia.* Notice he and his companions left *at once.* When an opportunity presented itself, Paul was ready to act. As a result, in Pisidian Antioch: *The word of the Lord spread through the whole region* (Acts 13:49). In Macedonia, he established key churches in Philippi, Thessalonica, Berea, and other places. Today, much of the good in orphanages, churches, businesses, and governments exists simply because someone chose to act and refused to shrink back or quit.

Yet many have failed to act in the past. We've hesitated. We haven't always moved forward with courage. Maybe we weren't ready. Could it be that now is the time? Is the time now ripe for the gifts you have to offer? Could it be the only thing stopping you is *you?*

If so, now may be your time. Today may be your day—the day to launch into the unknown waters. Plan as best you can, but head for the white water. Give it a shot. "Don't die wondering."

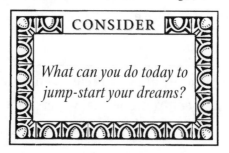

CONSIDER

What can you do today to jump-start your dreams?

10

Be One of Those People

As a prisoner for the Lord, then, I urge you to live
a life worthy of the calling you have received.

EPHESIANS 4:1

Periodically we encounter people whose lives speak louder than their words. They walk what they talk; they practice what they preach. They push the envelopes in their lives, and they don't settle for mediocrity. Instead they live for what they believe and usually bring others along in their wake.

One speaker referred to them as "those people." "Those people" incarnate an ideal and create legacies that last. Yes, "those people" are rare, but they are fully alive and live life to the fullest. They are proactive in how they approach their lives, rather than allowing their lives to dictate to them. I want to be that kind of person. How about you?

Paul realized an important principle of human development: People can choose whether or not they live up to their potential. It's possible to be blessed with incredible talent, skills, opportunity, and education, yet not accept one's identity. As an individual once challenged me, "Why are you driving like you're a rusted out Gremlin when God made you a Porsche?" In other words, don't accept a lower identity.

It's possible to be blessed with incredible
talent, skills, opportunity, and education,
yet not accept one's identity.

Paul regularly referred to others in a way that reflected their elevated identity in Christ: children of God, a chosen people, heirs. They had something to offer that the world needed because of the work of Christ in their lives.

Paul certainly was one of "those people." He didn't merely coast through life; he lived it to the fullest. He had a message to spread and a job to do. To know Paul was to know the Message. He was a man stunned by the love of God and who sacrificially offered his life as an example.

Fittingly, those invited to *live a life worthy of the calling* received the letter from Paul while he was imprisoned for his faith. *Be completely humble and gentle; be patient, bearing with one another in love* (Ephesians 4:2). It would have been difficult, or impossible, to take those words seriously if the author had given up when the going got tough. No, Paul didn't just share a message. He lived it. He knew it started with him.

Just this morning, I was invited to breakfast by two young business-men. As we became acquainted and shared stories, we realized that our lives had been impacted by the same man over the last ten years: Larry Clark. He was one of "those people." Unfortunately he tragically lost his life a few years ago in a bus accident. As we took turns sharing our experiences with Larry, we soon realized that he was a person we wanted to emulate. He believed in creating community among leaders and had done so for each of us. He saw a need and met it by making strategic connections. Even the fact that the three of us were together was the result of his influence.

Truly, the purest visions flow from deep within us. The greatest accomplishments result from what we're willing to model, or, possibly, what we can't help but model—our passions, desires, and gifts.

Paul envisioned a community of believers touched by grace and called to serve—people who would sacrifice for each other—a community like the one Jesus created with His disciples. He *did not come to be served, but to serve, and to give his life as a ransom for many* (Matthew 20:28). It was as if Paul had WWJD tattooed on his soul: What Would Jesus Do?

Our world is searching for leaders who will demonstrate a new way, who live out of conviction and inspire through their actions. Saint Francis of Assissi put it this way, "Preach the gospel. And if you must, use words." We've grown weary of those who say one thing and do another, yet we see this in our own lives and realize it's just not the way life is meant to be lived. There is a better way.

Our world is searching for leaders who will demonstrate a new way, who live out of conviction and inspire through their actions.

Don't undertake an endeavor just because it will make money and create jobs. Do it because you know the power of the product, because you've experienced the benefits yourself, and because you've seen it meet a need. As you embrace your role as chief proponent or point man, you will discover an inner strength and confidence will emerge—a motivation that will carry you through the darkest nights and the strongest rogue winds. With this confidence you can enter a certain rest as you observe the joy of others benefiting from your product or service. It is something you feel great about, because you've already tried it and it passed the test.

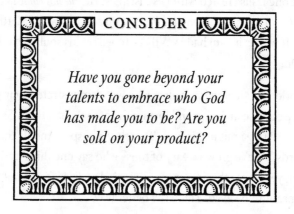

CONSIDER

Have you gone beyond your talents to embrace who God has made you to be? Are you sold on your product?

11

Let It Grow

I planted the seed, Apollos watered it, but God made it grow.

1 CORINTHIANS 3:6

Paul knew that sometimes his entrepreneurial work was just that—work. It required tedious labor and effort. *The Lord has assigned to each his task,* he wrote (1 Corinthians 3:5). Paul's task was to plant the seed. Metaphorically, he tilled soil, yanked weeds, broke rock, and scattered seed. You could say he made cold calls, followed up, addressed objections, and delivered product.

At times Paul's job required him to enlist the support of others. *Apollos watered it,* he wrote. In other words Apollos completed the intellectual spade work when Paul moved on. *While Apollos was at Corinth, Paul took the road through the interior and arrived at Ephesus* (Acts 19:1).

Though Paul's work was vital, he realized something every entrepreneurial leader must understand. There comes a time when we must simply let go of the outcome and trust the growing process. *God makes it grow,* Paul wrote. An element existed completely out of his control. This is "God stuff," divine work, the part that only God can do.

There comes a time when we must simply let go of the outcome and trust the growing process.

When I was eight years old, I conducted my own experiment in growth. I dug a hole next to our porch in New Jersey and gently placed some corn in the ground. I covered the seed with dirt. I watered it with a bucket and then watched—and watched—almost all day! Eventually, I planned to dig it all up but forgot about it. I went on to other things. I let it go. Then one day, almost as if by complete accident, I discovered this little green thing popping out of the soil where I had planted the seed. It was a miracle! The corn really did grow! There it was—my first corn stalk! I was a farmer. I sprinted into the house. "Mom, come see! Mom, come see! Look what *I* grew!"

When it comes to entrepreneurial growth, there is a time to work and a time to wait, a time to plant and a time to be patient, a time to invest and a time to rest. The writer of Ecclesiastes wrote, *[God] has made everything beautiful in its time* (Ecclesiastes 3:11).

Many of the best things in life require both space and time. Creativity requires time and leisure, solitude and rest, unhurried schedules, and uncluttered desks. A story told of Henry Ford is a good example. He was approached about an employee whose feet were up on a desk. "That man isn't working!"

"That man has made millions of dollars for me by not working," Ford replied.[26]

Often our times of relaxation and serenity produce our best ideas— when we're out for a run, working in a garden, or doing other things.

The ideas simply flow from deep within us, as if out of the clear blue. I've thought quite often about those words and those of leadership author Ken Blanchard who said at a conference in Boston, "I hardly remember ever writing *The One Minute Manager!* It was kind of a spiritual experience!"[27]

A best-selling book by Mihaly Csikszentmihalyi, describes the process he calls "flow." Athletes refer to this state as "the zone." It is a place of self-forgetfulness, where you quit ruminating and worrying; and become utterly absorbed in what you're doing. One composer described it this way:

> *You yourself are in an ecstatic state to such a point that you feel as though you almost don't exist. I've experienced this time and time again. My hand seems devoid of myself, and I have nothing to do with what's happening. I just sit there watching in a state of awe and wonderment. And it [the music] just flows by itself.*

In real life our best work, our best thinking, and our greatest creativity come when we are in a state of letting go, a totally relaxed state. We give up worrying about the product and we let God cause the growth. We go with the flow and enjoy the ride. We get in the groove.

> In real life our best work, our best thinking, and our greatest creativity come when we are in a state of letting go, a totally relaxed state.

Paul said, *I have learned the secret of being content in any and every situation* (Philippians 4:12). He did what he could, but then he let go of all the projects and prospects he could not influence or control. He did his part; he planted seeds—seeds that have been spread all over the world.

We may not see who plants the seeds, waters them, weeds the garden, or makes the seeds grow. We may not know who purchases our product, reads our books, carries out our vision, or builds the organization, but we can do our part—then stand back and watch things grow.

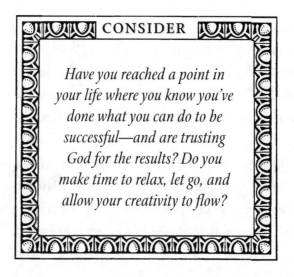

CONSIDER

Have you reached a point in your life where you know you've done what you can do to be successful—and are trusting God for the results? Do you make time to relax, let go, and allow your creativity to flow?

12

Lean into Your Passion

*While Paul was waiting for them in Athens, he was greatly
distressed to see that the city was full of idols.*

ACTS 17:16

Webster's dictionary defines *passion* as "an intense emotion compelling action." My computer thesaurus links it to words such as *desire, craving, fondness,* and *affection.*

You may not be used to talking about or even considering your passions; however, it is critical to the entrepreneurial leader. It's the engine that keeps us going, the atomic force we must harness. It's what keeps us thinking and overcoming obstacles long after others quit. It's the fuel that unleashes our creativity and the inspiration to enlist others.

It's what keeps us thinking and overcoming obstacles
long after others quit. It's the fuel that unleashes
our creativity and the inspiration to enlist others.

Author Lynne Hybels compares the value of engaging our passion to leaning into the wind when learning to windsurf. She describes sensing the invisible power of the wind but wondering if you can trust it. Just catch the wind and speed across the water, right? It sounds easy, but when you first get on the board, you try to control it with your legs as you stand; you wobble. The board is unstable and unsteady. As the wind blows, you become tense, clutching tighter until you begin to falter—and plop into the water.

The key to windsurfing is to trust in the invisible power of the wind: *lean into it!* You've spent many years believing that when you lean back too far, you fall; but *now* when the wind blows, you must lean into it. Trust the wind. Relax and don't try so hard to keep your balance. Trust the laws of gravity and the power of the wind.

Passions are like the invisible force of that wind. As Dr. Steve Lake says on the subject, "It gets your heart beating faster and your blood flowing swiftly through your arteries. It is the spiritual DNA embedded in the core of your being. It is the fading ember that bursts into flames with a sudden gust of wind."[28] When unleashed, it opens up enormous potential that we are just beginning to comprehend.

In windsurfing, as in life, there comes a time when you just need to take the risk and lean into it. You will discover the thing you're most passionate about. Go for it and stop apologizing. Many of us have been told (or have told ourselves) things like, "If it's what you *want* to do, then you can't call it *work*"; "Keep your passion in check"; "You might fall flat on your face, so play it safe." Whether education has forced it out of us or someone has told us to stay in the usual track, we stifle that which would release us to fly across the waves.

What stirs the embers inside of you?

Paul was passionate about people who didn't have any real connection with God. When he encountered their superstitions, he leaned into his passion and calling. He questioned what they were doing and why. And he shared his message: *The God who made the world and everything in it is the Lord of heaven and earth and does not live in temples built by hands* (Acts 17:24). The same intense man who set out to eradicate Christianity used his confrontational style to expose false gods and teach the truth.

Fan into flame the gift of God, which is in you" (2 Timothy 1:6). Lean into what's inside of you. Gifts and passions don't begin in full bloom; they must be put into use and continually developed. It's likely that you are already operating in your area of passion in some way. You probably can't help yourself. You are attracted to certain issues, people, or needs. Some conversations can keep you up all night. Certain situations galvanize you to action.

I have a friend who is passionate about the death penalty. He constantly sends me articles and information on the issue. He asks if I've given the issue any more consideration or if I've read any of the material he sent to me. He appeals to my sense of forgiveness. When we talk about this subject, his energy level soars.

My brother Todd is passionate about politics. He believes that a truly representative democracy requires more ordinary citizens to become involved in government; so he zealously campaigns for term limits. He chose not to run for another term himself, staying true to his conviction. Other people tell him he's committing political suicide, but he shrugs it off and leans into his passion.

Though they may not be immediately obvious to you, many of your passions were formed in your past. Some likely originated in your childhood. They may come from what Dr. Steve Lake calls peak experiences, times when you have really felt alive and excited about life.

Other passions may have been formed during your *pit* experiences—when you have experienced pain, loss, or grief. When you come out of the pit, your passion may be to show others the way out or how to avoid the pain altogether.

Maybe you find that certain things bug you, but don't bother others. Perhaps you become emotional or even teary-eyed by what leaves others cold. "Whenever you find tears in your eyes, especially unexpected tears, it is well to pay the closest attention," says author Fredrick Buechner[29] All these things are clues to your passion. Reflection on the peaks and pit—the stars and the scars—can cause you to discover your passion is written right into your own life story.

Reflection on the peaks and pit—the stars and the scars—can cause you to discover your passion is written right into your own life story.

I attended a conference where songwriter Ian Cron performed a song about people who never slow down long enough to find the deeper meaning of their lives. Cron described the "get-ahead traveler" with all the trappings of success but lacking an anchor for the soul. He described a friend after the event of September 11, beginning to wonder, "As you fly from Hong Kong through L.A. / I hope you see the clouds and say / Something more, I think there's something more."[30] That song touched something deep inside me and helped me to realize my own calling to unleash leaders to be free, fruitful, and focused.

One semi-discouraged, middle-aged businessman I was coaching asked me, "How can I know for sure? At my age and stage, I don't want to make a mistake and go down a rabbit trail."

"Well," I asked, "what gets you going? What are you excited about?"

"Health care," he replied. "I want to help health care become people-focused. It should be about meeting people's needs instead of being enslaved to the regulations of insurance programs." This was a genuine revelation of his passion.

Only you can know what that area of passion is for you. It can be risky. It may require great courage for you to lean into it. You may run the risk of rejection or the label of a fanatic. Some won't understand, but as you lean into it, you'll know it's right for you, and you'll wonder what held you back before. "To live is the rarest thing in the world," said Oscar Wilde. Most people exist, that is all."[31] It may be time for you to fly.

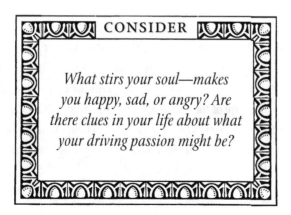

CONSIDER

What stirs your soul—makes you happy, sad, or angry? Are there clues in your life about what your driving passion might be?

13

Be Accountable

*On arriving there, they gathered the church together
and reported all that God had done through them.*

ACTS 14:27

Many entrepreneurial leaders don't want a boss. They've been there, done that—bought the T-shirt, sold the T-shirt, even designed the T-shirt—for someone else. When most entrepreneurs ask why they went out on their own, the most common response is, "I wanted to be my own boss."

Being your own boss does have its perks: flexible hours, freedom to try out your own ideas, the power to do things your way. It's great! Right? Sure it is—until the creative risk-taker-types get mired in an organizational bottleneck, begin to run off on tangents, or begin new things before finishing any of the things they've already started. Like most do with their New Year's resolutions, we entrepreneurs tend to forget our goals. Deadlines start to slip, and to keep it all going, we work ourselves into the ground to get it all done!

As crazy as it may seem, many entrepreneurial leaders don't follow a plan but embrace the "wing and a prayer" method. The bad new is that over 80 percent of small businesses fail within the first five years.

As Michael Gerber points out in *The E-Myth*, 80 percent of the small businesses that survive the first five years fail in the second five! What's an entrepreneur to do?

It would have been very easy for Paul to be a maverick missionary—accountable to no one and totally on his own. Although he was commissioned and sent by the church at Antioch, they had a limited ability to keep track of Paul as he traveled from one remote region to another. But Paul chose to be accountable.

Something healthy takes place when we realize we are not alone, that others care about us and are interested in what we're doing. Although they can't be on the front lines with us day to day, they play a key role on our team. They act as sounding boards, celebrate with us when things go well, console us when things get rough, and point out areas that need attention.

Something healthy takes place when we realize we are not alone, that others care about us and are interested in what we're doing.

Wisely, Paul didn't continue to move from outpost to outpost. Instead, in the Book of Acts we see that Paul and his partner Barnabas returned to the city of Antioch and gathered the church together. *They . . . reported all that God had done through them and how he had opened the door of faith to the Gentiles* (Acts 14:27). Although minutes from their "board meetings" don't exist today, one wonders what they discussed. They probably provided a personal update on how they were doing spiritually, emotionally, and physically. Likely they also spoke about the status of their mission.

Acts records that after they reported back, *They stayed there a long time with the disciples* (Act 14:28). Can you imagine why? Could it be that after spending so much time on the front lines, they longed for the safety and support of those who believed in them? They might have simply enjoyed being with those who wanted to share the ups and downs of their mission, the victories and the struggles. That's what real accountability provides. It offers encouragement and sustenance. It says, "We want you to succeed." To the entrepreneurial leader, accountability can offer an oasis of understanding from those to whom you are accountable.

I believe that accountability (sometimes in the form of coaching) is the electricity that empowers an entrepreneurial leader's greatest accomplishments. This book is a perfect example. I learned that the publisher wanted the manuscript by a particular day in the not-so-distant future, so I sat at Starbucks, pen in hand, a cup of coffee and a notebook by my side. For months, the pen lay dormant. Now, I'm being held accountable, and, quite honestly, it feels good. Accountability can make an entrepreneur feel like he or she is finally in gear and going somewhere.

I recently asked Jerry Pinney, who teaches classes on entrepreneurial planning, what most often is the "make it or break it" difference? Without hesitation, he shot back, "Accountability—it's crucial."

"What do you mean?" I asked.

"If you're a one-person operation, or the main one responsible, you must find someone to keep you accountable and focused—a board of advisors, a board of directors, a coach, a small group of other entrepreneurs." He continued, "The reason you did so well in school was that you had elements to hold you accountable—a test, a teacher, Mom and Dad. You still need that kind of outside obligation."

If you want your mission to succeed, find someone to hold you accountable and give them permission to do so. Then when you need to report or be reminded of your mission, goals, and strategies, you won't be on your own. Encourage questions about your focus, resource management, and even your health. Then be willing to give them permission to offer what Pastor Bill Hybels calls "the other 10 percent." That's the extra-hard stuff they might want to ask, but because of the perceived risk of offending you, they don't. Sometimes the things that remain unsaid can prove to be your undoing. Jesus said, *The truth will set you free* (John 8:32). The same principle applies to accountability.

If you want your mission to succeed,
find someone to hold you accountable
and give them permission to do so.

The commitment of another to ask, "How's it going?" can keep you from becoming stagnant. It can keep you from allowing your own entrepreneurial fever to move you on to the next great idea before you sufficiently work through the great idea at hand. Even input that may sound critical or even ignorant can help you avoid needless heartache or financial blunders.

Paul and Barnabas knew their need for accountability. They traveled hundreds of miles in order to get it. You need it too. It might be weekly, monthly, quarterly, or annually. Whether it's from a board, a group, or a coach, accountability and feedback is vital. At first it may feel uncomfortable, but eventually you will look forward to simple questions like, "How's it going?" Then you'll be able to share the *real* concerns, and you'll begin to find real answers. In fact, you might just find the wind that will fill your sails and keep you going for the long haul.

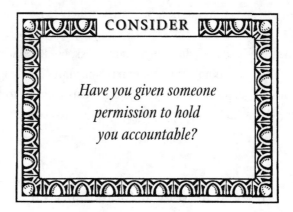

CONSIDER

Have you given someone permission to hold you accountable?

14

Learn Contentment

I have learned to be content whatever the circumstances.

PHILIPPIANS 4:11

How well do you handle the roller coasters, the doors that seem to open one day only to slam shut the next, the flourish of activity, and the waiting it out? How do you cope with the "Yes, of course!" one moment and the "No, not interested." the next?

In 1992, I checked into a monastery in Cambridge, Massachusetts, and arranged a meeting with a monk named Brother John. "Brother John," I began. "Things I've planned lately just haven't gone my way."

He listened quietly and then smiled knowingly. "Jeff, I've been in ministry for forty years now, and never—well maybe once—have things ever really gone the way I planned them. Does God need you to keep His universe going smoothly? It's okay, Jeff. Just relax. Relax."

In his book *Emotional Intelligence,* Daniel Goleman shares that the way we deal with our emotions is almost more important than what we know in our heads. He writes, "A sense of self-mastery, of being able to withstand the emotional storms that the buffeting of fortune brings rather than being 'passion's slaves' has been praised as a virtue since the time of Plato . . . . Indeed, keeping our distressing emotions in check is the key to emotional well-being."[32]

Regardless of professions, we all need emotional stability, but emotional fitness is a nonnegotiable item for entrepreneurial leaders. It's part of the job to keep your inner self calm yet passionate, despite the storms of startup. You can't afford seasons of discouragement, despair, or dissatisfaction. Just as you must keep your body healthy and fit, you must keep your inner self healthy, fit, and hopeful.

Sometimes it's a fight to maintain emotional health. A variety of things can hit, and we soon find ourselves in personal combat. While we'd rather enlist someone else to do it for us, the fight for contentment is ours alone. Speaking on this topic, Bill Hybels said, "Every man who consistently displays a positive attitude has fought for it. Repeat after me," he invited. "Whose job is it to maintain a positive attitude? Repeat after me," he invited again, *"That's my job.* Whose job? *That's my job."*[33]

Paul knew that maintaining an emotional balance was essential to inner well-being. He taught that one of his most valuable secrets was that he had learned to be content. Whether facing blue sky or dark clouds, perspective comes from the inside. He stated, *I know what it is to be in need, and I know what it is to have plenty. I have learned the secret of being content in any and every situation, whether well fed or hungry, whether living in plenty or in want* (Philippians 4:12).

Now it's one thing to hear such a testimony from someone living in luxury and obvious success—"Of course you're content! Who wouldn't be if they had what you have?"—but how do you encourage others to be content while languishing in a lonely prison cell? That's what Paul did. While enduring incredibly difficult circumstances, he maintained a positive mental attitude and wrote others, encouraging them to endure their suffering patiently. While facing financial hardships and even shipwreck, he described himself as *rich.* Writing to the Corinthian church, he related that he moved on *in troubles, hardships and distresses; in beatings, imprisonments and riots; in hard work, sleepless nights and hunger; . . . known, yet regarded as unknown; dying, and yet we live on; beaten, and yet not killed* (2 Corinthians 6:4-5, 9-10).

Paul practiced vigilance of the mind. He captured the darker thoughts and replaced them with positive ones. He refused anxiety, and wouldn't let discouragement fester. He fought for hope. He took *captive every thought* (2 Corinthians 10:5). *Rejoice in the Lord always* (Philippians 4:4), he told the Philippians. Train your mind to think positive, life-giving thoughts.

Still, some of us learn through pain. I put myself in this category. "Mindy," I would say to my wife, "I'm really frustrated." Then I would rehearse my woes and challenges. Although I thought I was only admitting reality, I actually created reality for myself. Weeks and months of continual complaints and discontentment eventually led to what was later diagnosed as chronic depression. I simmered over things that weren't going my way. I painted worst-case scenarios. The price I paid for sagging emotional fitness was enormous. My inner-gloom negatively affected my marriage, my health, and my children. Even I didn't like living with me. Recovery took years.

Slowly, with practice, we can learn to stop discontentment before it takes hold. We can nip it in the bud. "No, I'm not going to go there." For example, you must decide that financial downturns won't define you. Client no's must be seen as part of the game. Employees who quit should be seen as an opportunity to fill a position with someone who's an even better fit. We can replace fearful thinking with faith as a discipline. And do you know what happens? We start to see light streaming back into the darkness. We notice opportunities when we quit focusing on setbacks. Paul's letter to the Philippians has taught me many helpful lessons in this battle.

Slowly, with practice, we can learn to stop discontentment before it takes hold.

Paul encouraged the Philippians, *Do not be anxious about anything, but in everything, by prayer and petition, with thanksgiving, present your requests to God* (Philippians 4:6). Don't be anxious about *anything*. Nothing. Instead, replace anxious thoughts with positive ideas. Seek wise counsel for feedback. Consider turning to prayer. You can always tell God what you need. You may have never thought about it before, but God is even bigger than any need you've ever had or will have.

Sometimes it's even helpful to perform a cost/benefit analysis of our fear and worry. Try it. Write on a piece of paper, "What if I just continue to worry and be anxious over this? What will it cost me?" You're likely to write words like *discouragement, damage, bad decisions,* and *depression.* Then list the benefits. You're likely to come up with an empty list.

The discipline of positive thinking seems to come easier for some than others, but you are capable of creating your own environment of emotional health and intelligence. Like Paul, you can be content. Make one decision at a time not to sweat the small stuff. Make one choice to hold off and not lose your cool. One moment of acceptance and serenity will build upon another.

The discipline of positive thinking seems to come easier for some than others, but you are capable of creating your own environment of emotional health and intelligence.

Don't buy into the lie that you're cursed and doomed by what's going on around you. There is an alternative.

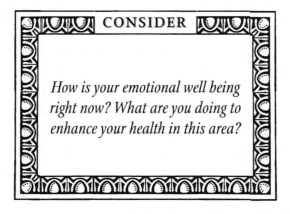

CONSIDER

How is your emotional well being right now? What are you doing to enhance your health in this area?

15

Keep Growing

Our light and momentary troubles are achieving
for us an eternal glory that far outweighs them all.

2 CORINTHIANS 4:17

Paul realistically recognized that his toil and hardships took a toll on him physically and emotionally. His body weakened and his afflictions continued. The hours were long and the pay practically nonexistent.

The Christian movement was experiencing obvious growth, but Paul was mature enough to realize that growth is not just an external thing. Another, more profound type of growth was also taking place—inner growth, spiritual maturity. *We do not lose heart* (2 Corinthians 4:1), Paul wrote to the church in Corinth. Although few would have blamed him if he had lost heart, Paul recognized a benefit resulted from his challenges. *Though outwardly we are wasting away, yet inwardly we are being renewed day by day* (2 Corinthians 4:16). The result was resilience. Paul recognized that his spiritual being grew, even when his physical energies were diminishing.

If Paul were to teach a class on entrepreneurial leadership today, I don't think he would lay out the ten-step strategy to success or the fifty leadership to-dos. Instead, I believe he would encourage spiritual growth. I can imagine him saying something like, "Don't just focus on outward growth. Grow internally. Who you become is even more important than what you do."

As Jesus taught, *What good will it be for a man if he gains the whole world, yet forfeits his soul?* (Matthew 16:26). Your personal growth as a leader produces a lasting prosperity and legacy that is solid and worthwhile; its effects are enormous, and it will endure after you are gone.

Your personal growth as a leader produces a lasting prosperity and legacy that is solid and worthwhile; its effects are enormous, and it will endure after you are gone.

When Paul wrote letters to other leaders, he didn't lay out pat answers. Instead he shared his experiences in the furnace of life and encouraged others to press on. He taught that it was possible to grow in and maintain inner peace, perspective, and wholeness—even under pressure.

As a leader, your influence comes from *you*. Although few leadership books teach you how to attain greater love, joy, peace, patience, and kindness, Paul's plan for leadership development didn't leave these out. If we take even small steps in this direction, the world becomes a better, kinder place; and our organizations do too. Ultimately people want to follow leaders who continue to change and grow. We're attracted to people who learn from their mistakes and even admit when they're wrong. Transparency builds trust and confidence.

One CEO I coach shared that his main goal for the year was *not* just to grow the company. His main goal was to learn how to lead his company in a new way. "I don't want to keep pushing people to just do more," he said. "This year, I want to find out how to lead the company without all the stress, anxiety, and control. I want to learn what it means to allow God to lead my company."

To some this might sound kind of crazy. Some might say it's downright fanatical. I don't see it that way. Frankly, I believe my CEO friend is discovering that spirituality and business are not necessarily two separate endeavors. He's no longer willing to segment his life into secular and sacred. It's *all* sacred. Just as organizations are made up of people, leaders are a composite of what's written on their souls. What Paul teaches is at the core of leadership development. We will influence most significantly through what is found in our inner selves. When our inner selves are changing, growing, and finding purpose, peace, and perspective, guess what happens to the organization?

Paul teaches that hardships and setbacks can accelerate profound inner growth like nothing else. In his own story, he shares, *We are hard pressed on every side, but not crushed; perplexed, but not in despair; persecuted, but not abandoned; struck down, but not destroyed* (2 Corinthians 4:8). Certainly Paul does not advocate denial. He experienced times when it was just tough going, plain and simple, but Paul remained committed to continued growth. He concluded, *we do not lose heart. Though outwardly we are wasting away, yet inwardly we are being renewed day by day. For our light and momentary troubles are achieving for us an eternal glory that far outweighs them all* (2 Corinthians 4:16-17). Growth is a process, not a one-time event.

When we're in the midst of troubles, most of them don't feel *light and momentary.* The football team goes through wind sprints and intense sessions of lifting before the games begin. The men grasp for breath and wonder if they can push it for one more repetition, but every player is glad he went through the pain when it's game time. Soldiers curse rigorous basic training but then appreciate it when real combat begins.

> The men grasp for breath and wonder if they can push it for one more repetition, but every player is glad he went through the pain when it's game time.

Growth requires us to stretch ourselves. "What doesn't kill you can make you better," says one Marine slogan. Another reads, "Pain is just weakness leaving the body." The value of such growth may elude you at times. You weren't educated and trained to think about your inner self. You were encouraged to seek achievements, accolades, and right actions. You learned that it was good to care for your body, to stay mentally and physically fit; but who mentored you in how to develop a tough yet tender inner self?

Your job is, according to Frederick Buechner, to "Listen to your life." Find the deeper meanings of what is going on and keep growing. Learn and stretch. Buechner continues, "See it for the fathomless mystery that it is. In the boredom and the pain of it no less than in the excitement and gladness; touch, taste, smell your way to the holy and hidden heart of it because in the last analysis all moments are key moments."[34] Don't allow yourself to become stagnant in this aspect of your growth. Let your challenges develop inner resilience, toughness, and tenderness. Allow the momentary troubles to form you and shape you. As you do, others will seek you out for your wisdom. Your soul as well as your influence will expand.

> ## CONSIDER
>
> *What might be the situation or challenge that is causing or affecting the greatest inner growth in you right now? What good may come from it? If what Paul wrote is true* (Our light and momentary troubles are achieving for us an eternal glory that far outweighs them all.), *how might it affect the way you handle adversity this week?*

16

Let Go of the Reins

I commit you to God and to the word of his grace.

ACTS 20:32

"Should I hold on tight or just let go?" Entrepreneurial leaders wrestle with this question all the time. The writer of the Old Testament book of Ecclesiastes had keen insight: *There is a time for everything . . . a time to be born and a time to die, a time to plant and a time to uproot, a time to kill and a time to heal, a time to tear down and a time to build* (Eccelsiastes 3:1-3). There are seasons in life.

How do we know when it's time to let go? What time is it now? Time rarely comes with a label. Imagine a voice that says: "Now is the time to invest"; "Now is the time to hire"; "Now is the time to retire." For the entrepreneurial leader, it might be helpful to have a warning signal that says, "Now is the time to stop doing the work yourself and let others take over."

Paul didn't wrestle with or panic over timing. He seemed to understand this concept. At times he settled in and waited; at other times he moved on. Sometimes he did the work himself; other times he released the work to others. He knew when to engage himself in an endeavor and when to delegate.

Paul had a good sense of timing. He actively decentralized leadership and empowered the Church to swell beyond the ranks of a tiny minority sect. Neither Paul nor the other apostles became bottle-necks to growth. They believed in a leadership model that started things, drew in others, equipped them, then let them take over the reins. Then the leaders moved on to the next challenge.

Without the benefits of modern communication, this continual "letting go and turning over" church-growth model spread from Jerusalem to Asia Minor, to Africa, Europe, and beyond. The ministry quickly expanded beyond their reach and crossed borders, cultures, and continents. Churches were planted, and new networks of leaders sprung up everywhere. Like a living organism, leadership teams grew, divided, and multiplied. Apostles entrusted new leaders with authority and responsibility. New foundations were laid, and new leaders were drawn into leadership. Paul then willingly moved on to new terri-tory—leaving others to run what his team had started. Even when he was in prison, things continued to grow.

In a world that highly esteems executive and managerial leadership, the challenge to hold things loosely seems to assault our pride and egos. "I started this thing! Why should I let others have a say? It's mine! It was my hard work! These are my ideas." It's tough on our egos when others come along and don't even know who we are. What if they're better at some of those things than we are? Are we willing to let them do them? Are we confident enough in our own calling to let others lead in theirs?

In a world that highly esteems executive and managerial leadership, the challenge to hold things loosely seems to assault our pride and egos.

Paul didn't hold things with a clenched fist. Generously, and seemingly without much fuss, he gave over leadership and responsibility. Knowing who he was and who he wasn't, he willingly let go and entrusted others with responsibilities. He wasn't called to be a church elder, so he enlisted and trained those who were. He wasn't a pastor, so he drew in people with that calling. He wrote to the leaders of the Ephesian church, *Now I commit you to God and to the word of his grace* (Acts 20:32).

Let go of control. Why is that so hard for many leaders to do? One reason leaders have difficulty letting go is that the model of leadership we've traditionally been given is one of management—not entrepreneurial leadership. Although the managerial style of leadership is valid, it isn't the only one. In contrast to it, entrepreneurial leadership lays foundations, frequently built upon by others.

The second reason it's hard is that most leaders view their work as their own baby. They had the dream and were there at the birth. They've invested in the outcome, financially and emotionally. They want nothing but the best for *their* baby. They can't imagine that anyone else can really raise their baby or even take a primary role in its education or training. But to allow for growth, we need to let others lead too. The truth is, the new people may not be as qualified or as passionate as we have been over an endeavor, but when it's time to pass the baton, we need to do it and move on.

Over the years I've wrestled with this entrepreneurial dilemma, and I've spoken with others who have as well. "When have I done all I can do? When is it time to let go? When it is time to let someone else take the helm?"

"When have I done all I can do? When is it time to let go? When it is time to let someone else take the helm?"

A few years ago, I became convinced that I needed to step back from direct leadership of Beacon Community Church in Boston. I had been part of starting and leading it for almost nine years. In order to move on, I had to know that it was right for me and for the church. My inner voices screamed, "Are you crazy? You'll lose control! No one cares as much as you do! You'll lose prestige. No one will ever even remember that you worked so hard to found this!" My "What ifs?" had an argument with my "Why nots?" But those who knew me best, including my wife, agreed that it was time to turn over the reins. Others were ready and wanted to lead. It was the right direction to go.

I usually don't receive such dramatic signs, but that time I felt like I needed it. I needed confirmation that if I entrusted "my baby" to the hands of others, it would be okay. Somehow, after that day, I knew it would survive, maybe even thrive, and I was confident I would not regret my decision. Two years later, the church is thriving under the leadership of a team doing an outstanding job.

I understand that for you, letting go of the reins may not mean as drastic a step as leaving a significant leadership role. It may simply mean doing things differently, such as refusing to micromanage or do it all yourself. If you are called to entrepreneurial leadership, you must learn the art of letting go. It's vital to your health and to your soul.

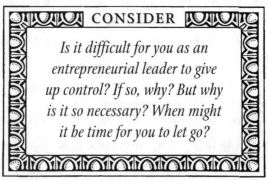

CONSIDER

Is it difficult for you as an entrepreneurial leader to give up control? If so, why? But why is it so necessary? When might it be time for you to let go?

17

Give It a Rest!

On the Sabbath we went outside the city gate to the river.

ACTS 16:13

"Exhausted," read the headline in *Time Magazine* in 1994. Behind it was the picture of Harvard University's weary president, Neil Rudenstein. Under the weight of enormous responsibility and the relentless pace of his work, Rudenstein finally collapsed. His doctor's prescription: "Spend time away." Realizing his level of chronic over-work demanded more than a few good nights of sleep, his doctor rec-ommended he leave Cambridge and head off to a quiet island, removed from the pace and responsibilities.[35] He did what he should have been doing all along—he took a break and got away.

In a day when we are hit with an unrelenting barrage of information, constant access, and new opportunities, it's important to counteract "lifestyles without margins" and the tendency to live in overdrive. "I always feel like I have to do more," says my friend Jim who leads a cutting-edge department in a large organization.

"Some of us start to feel like road-kill on the information superhigh-way," said author Gordon MacDonald speaking to graduate students at MIT in Cambridge.[36] Stores are open around the clock. The Internet is always available. *Shouldn't we keep going,* we wonder?

Paul knew better. Although he had churches to oversee, messages to preach, new territories to reach, and leaders to develop, when the Sabbath came, Paul headed *outside the city gate to the river* (Acts 16:13). I can just imagine him strolling along the water's edge as he withdrew from the hustle and bustle and sought tranquility outside the city gates.

Do you realize that sometimes the best demonstration of faith is evidenced by the work we *don't* do? We all have to guard against laziness and procrastination, but more often than not, we need to place healthy boundaries around our work. We exercise faith when we let go of control. We can experience a divine rest trusting that what we have started will continue. As my mentor and friend Jerome says, "It's all God's work anyway, isn't it?"

We all have to guard against laziness and procrastination, but more often than not, we need to place healthy boundaries around our work. We exercise faith when we let go of control.

With this philosophy, we must loosen our grip and free our minds from strategizing and obsessing. We must get out of the way physically, mentally, and spiritually. We must trust and believe that, as the psalmist says, *Unless the LORD builds the house, its builders labor in vain*

(Psalm 127:1). He further elaborates, *In vain you rise up early and stay up late, toiling for food to eat—for [God] grants sleep to those he loves* (v. 2).

After thousands of years, the Jewish people still hold firmly to the Sabbath, a day of rest ceasing from work. They hold to the belief that even when they are not working, God's work continues. It's not all up to us. A divine hand waters the crops and grows the seeds. He protects investments and orchestrates plans for the future. He continues to carry out the mission.

To illustrate, during his getaway Paul encountered a group of women that was part of the divine plan. They had gathered to discuss spiritual matters when Paul *just happened* to meet them. One of those women, Lydia, would later become a great proponent of the Christian message throughout the region. *The Lord opened her heart to respond to Paul's message* (Acts 16:14). Paul didn't have to work to make this happen. It was part of the work God had already put into motion. Paul just joined in.

Rest and real productivity are related. As you develop a rhythm between engagement and disengagement, you are able to bring a healthy and complete you to your endeavors. When you spend time by the river, you return to the city refreshed and energized.

Rest and real productivity are related. As you develop a rhythm between engagement and disengagement, you are able to bring a healthy and complete you to your endeavors.

Rest can feel like an intrusion. You reason, *I'll just make a few calls* or *I'll just check my e-mail.* You wonder, *Can I afford to take time off?* Time away feels like a luxury, a waste of valuable time. Sometimes we feel antsy just sitting still for a few minutes, let alone a few days. Our minds buzz with ideas and to-do lists that beckon us. Words like, *Be still, and know that I am God* (Psalm 46:10) sound like relics from an ancient and outdated world. Be still? How?

Author Henri Nouwen writes candidly to those of us who find slowing down difficult: "When we have removed our outer distractions, we often find that our inner distractions manifest themselves in full force." He likens this quieting to the:

> . . . *experience of a man who, after years of living with open doors, suddenly decides to shut them. The visitors who used to come and enter his home start pounding on his doors, wondering why they are not allowed to enter. Only when they realize that they are not welcome do they gradually stop coming. This is the experience of anyone who decides to enter solitude after a life without much spiritual discipline. At first, the many distractions keep presenting themselves. Later, as they receive less and less attention, they slowly withdraw.*[37]

It is essential that we outlive this pounding if we are to come to a place of inner serenity. It will become easier as we accept that it's ultimately *not* up to us. Paul wrote, *I planted the seed, Apollos watered it, but God made it grow* (1 Corinthians 3: 6). This principle seems to contradict the accepted formula for success and our frenzied work ethic, yet *unless the LORD builds the house, its builders labor in vain* (Psalm 127:1). Paul believed this and acted accordingly. He took time away.

Be daring. Head out to the river and watch its constant flow. Enjoy nature, art, culture, hobbies, or friendships. Turn off the cell phone, and turn down the volume on your answering machine. Refuse to check your e-mail and even turn off the computer. Spend time with your family. Enjoy recreation and restore your body physically. Read a novel to rest your mind. Walk in a park or hike in the mountains to restore your soul. Stroll along a deserted beach. Breathe deeply the cool night air and enjoy the stars; and don't apologize, even to yourself.

As you consciously invest in time away, you will develop a rhythmic pace that will become a beacon to others. The more you realize that ultimately it is God who does the work and you are merely one of the players, you will be able to put anxiety aside and experience genuine rest. You can prevent the headline "Exhausted" from being emblazoned on your chest, and you will experience greater creativity, energy, and endurance.

Work hard, yes, but rest hard too. Both are important.

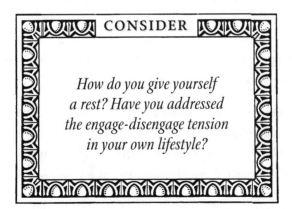

CONSIDER

*How do you give yourself
a rest? Have you addressed
the engage-disengage tension
in your own lifestyle?*

18

Release Resentments

Bear with each other and forgive whatever
grievances you may have against one another.

COLOSSIANS 3:13

A number of years ago, my brother Todd discovered a greenish, toxic rust flowing underground from an auto junkyard, making its way into a stream, then flowing through our backyard on its way to a lake. Although no one had noticed it before, it quickly became apparent that the relics of this ancient metal were polluting our water supply and possibly affecting our health. With the approval of a town commission, the ultimate solution became obvious: clear away the junkyard, dig up the decomposing cars, and remove the source of this hazardous waste. Sooner was better than later.

Like this buried waste, unresolved tensions make their way to the surface in our lives and affect our leadership. *Resentment* is defined by Webster's Dictionary as "a sense of injury or anger arising from a sense of wrong." It can stifle us and create harm in and through us.

According to *The Twelve Steps: A Spiritual Journey,* "Holding on to resentment causes stress, anxiety, and uncontrollable feelings of anger. If these are unresolved, serious emotional and physical consequences will develop . . . . Resentment doesn't punish anyone but ourselves. We can't hold resentments and find healing at the same time."[38]

What does releasing resentment have to do with the work of an entrepreneurial leader? Resentments take the breath out of our work and can actually dull our vision. They zap our energy and steal the enjoyment of working with others. They build up over time and rarely dissipate on their own. Scientists now tell us that long-term resentment and anger may eventually deplete necessary serotonin in our brains, leading to memory loss, an inability to make decisions, and depression.[39]

Resentments take the breath out of our work and can actually dull our vision. They zap our energy and steal the enjoyment of working with others. They build up over time and rarely dissipate on their own.

Such effects weigh us down and keep us from effectiveness in our mission. They sabotage our own well-being, wreaking havoc in our key relationships, health, and spiritual lives. We just can't afford for the toxin of resentment to continue to flow through our veins.

When we feel injured, angered, or wronged, we must learn to proactively release our resentments. As we get close to clients, teammates, or others we depend on, we will eventually be let down. Their junk will seep into the soil of our souls, and their flaws will touch us. This is nothing new. We've all been hurt in the past by parents, partners, or spouses. We've been let down by those who said, "Trust me." We've all felt rejected or abandoned at times.

Paul isn't naive about the way people treat even those trying to help them. His advice: *Forgive as the Lord forgave you* (Colossians 3:13). Then Paul offers himself as an example. Writing to Timothy, his protégé, Paul confesses his own resentments, *Alexander the metalworker did me a great deal of harm,* yet Paul's trusting response was *The Lord will repay him for what he has done* (2 Timothy 4:14). Elsewhere, likely referring to the same Alexander, Paul says, *Some have rejected these [instructions in grace] and so have shipwrecked their faith. Among them are Hymenaeus and Alexander* (1 Timothy 1:19-20).

Paul also knew what it was like to be abandoned by those he trusted. He said, *At my first defense, no one came to my support, but everyone deserted me.* In other words, when accused and brought to trial, Paul's friends were nowhere to be found! Yet, unwilling to allow resentment to gain a foothold, Paul released it, *May it not be held against them* (2 Timothy 4:16).

There's no denial here. Paul felt the pain of rejection, abandonment, and mistreatment. He put his all on the line, and others acted as fair-weather friends. Yet almost in the same breath, Paul released it. He forgave. He turned the wrongdoing of others over to God. He even went as far as to request their acquittal! *May it not be held against them.*

Sometimes we all need a safe place to share our anger and hurt. You may want to tell a close friend, a minister, a coach, or counselor. You may want to take your resentments and share them with God. If you read the Book of Psalms, you will discover this is a valid form of prayer—maybe even a kind of spiritual therapy! Admit your hurts and wounds, then seek healing and maybe a clean up crew. Confess your anger and let it go.

This is simple, but it isn't easy. Forgive. Consciously let go of a need to get even. Set your adversary free and abandon the desire to retaliate. You must forgive, not because you feel like forgiving, but because you need it for your own sense of well-being. Deliberately choose to absolve and move on—even if the offender doesn't deserve it! You may never receive an acknowledgment of the wrongdoing or an apology, but you have to move on.

You must forgive, not because you feel
like forgiving, but because you need it
for your own sense of well-being.

Although few consultants address this problem directly, good relationships and teamwork can conquer the toughest obstacles. Our teammates can help us weather financial storms or slumps in our productivity. On the other hand, poor relationships filled with resentment, hurt, and unresolved conflict quickly erode trust and wreak havoc on what we want to accomplish. Hostility spreads like a virus from one person to the next. It's not only a strategic problem, but a personal one. It involves the inner-workings of leadership.

"The primary battle is with the inner enemy," wrote Frances Wickes in *The Inner World of Choices.* "Until a man has conquered in himself that which causes hate, he contributes, consciously or unconsciously to the warfare of the world."[40]

Resentments zap our energy. On the contrary, inner healing and the freedom it engenders will release some of the greatest creativity in us. We must allow our inner core to heal and stop trying to prove something. As Paul taught, *As far as it depends on you, live at peace with everyone* (Romans 12:18).

As long as we deny the existence of our resentments and refuse to confess that we've harbored bitterness, we are held captive. However, when we choose to step out of denial and let our resentments go, we open the door to our own freedom.

This may or may not be where you are right now. If it's not, tuck this away in your head and pull it out when you need it. If this is an issue for you, take some good advice. Get to the heart of the matter and pluck that resentment out of the ground—ASAP. Then walk in freedom.

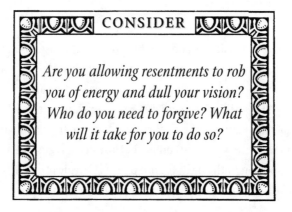

CONSIDER

Are you allowing resentments to rob you of energy and dull your vision? Who do you need to forgive? What will it take for you to do so?

19

See the Opportunity

King Agrippa, I consider myself fortunate to stand before you today.

ACTS 26:2

In his book, *Innovation and Entrepreneurship,* Peter Drucker writes, "Not much more than a century ago, neither mineral oil seeping out of the ground nor bauxite, the ore of aluminum, were resources. They were nuisances; both render the soil infertile. The penicillin mold was a pest, not a resource . . . . The overwhelming majority of successful innovations exploit change . . . and thus the discipline of innovation."[41]

Entrepreneurial leaders see such latent opportunity and exploit it. Today, we can't ignore the genius of these now famous visionaries who wondered if the waste products of oil and penicillin could be useful. At the time, almost everyone else merely considered them waste. *Waste* is "excess material or by-product, rejected as useless and worthless; refuse," according to Webster's Dictionary. Only a handful saw opportunity; however, they applied their curiosity, imaginations, creativity, and resources. They did something others wouldn't, and as a result, countless lives have benefited from their efforts.

Paul, too, modeled a lifestyle where such challenging opportunities were exploited for the good. While a prisoner, Paul was thrust in front of King Agrippa, the ruler of a vast area near the Sea of Galilee. Paul was forced to offer his defense in front of the influential ruler. Instead of fearfully seeing King Agrippa as a threat, however, Paul saw an opportunity for influence. He shared his story of moving from hostility to one of embracing the Christian message.

Of his mindset before his conversion, he said, *In my obsession against them, I even went to foreign cities to persecute them* (Act 26:11). Identifying with the likely objections of his target audience, Paul then shared why he had made the transition from a biased opponent to one of Christianity's most vocal advocates. He then moved boldly to close the deal: *King Agrippa, do you believe the prophets? I know you do* (Acts 26:27).

Astonished by Paul's nerve, Agrippa responds, *Do you think that in such a short time you can persuade me to be a Christian?* (v. 28).

We don't know the ultimate outcome of Paul's encounter with Agrippa that day. Nonetheless it's hard to miss Paul's gutsy willingness to turn a sticky situation into an opportunity to advance his cause. Instead of seeing Agrippa as a prosecutor, Paul saw a platform.

"Opportunities are seldom labeled," said John A. Shedd, but we can train ourselves to look for them. You may have heard the slogan, "When a door closes, look for a window." The entrepreneurial leadership principle Paul modeled in this situation was a willingness to look for windows. In your case, it is unlikely that you will appear before an official as a convicted criminal; nevertheless, be alert for opportunities:

- where change is taking place and new needs are arising,
- as demographics change,
- when there is a shift in the mood or thinking of people,

- where new knowledge or technology can be exploited,
- where untapped potential can be maximized, and
- in tough situations.

Sometimes opportunities are present when something really bugs you. As a personal coach, I've realized my own need to explore more closely what's bugging my clients. I help them look for clues to what exists on a deeper level or even help them see opportunities they might be missing.

"Why does that get under your skin so much?" I'll ask. "Could this be an opportunity for you to learn?" "Might this be a clue to your own calling to do something about the problem? Maybe it's a peek into your motivation?" In my own life, I've heard myself say things like, "Why doesn't someone do something about this?" But I've learned to ask the next question: "Might that someone be me? If I'm the one bugged by the matter seeping from underground, maybe I should take a closer look at it."

Other opportunities may exist right under your nose. For example, one woman who runs a photography business loves horses almost more than she loves cameras.

"Have you thought about taking pictures of horses?" I asked her.

"Actually, a number of people have talked to me about doing horse portraits," she said. "Maybe I should let people know I can do this."

The challenge for many of us is to not let our pace or our present mindset keep us from recognizing opportunities. Sometimes we need to step back to gain new perspective. It may be difficult to see opportunity in the midst of adversity. A client leaves, and we feel abandoned. A market shuts down, and we feel trapped. The economy slows, and we feel cursed. Yet seeing opportunities invites us to view our present challenges as pregnant with possibility.

The challenge for many of us is to not let our pace or our present mindset keep us from recognizing opportunities. Sometimes we need to step back to gain new perspective.

In your current landscape there are clues to new inventions, systems, and strategies. Consider these examples: The inventor of Silly Putty wondered what good could come out of a cream-colored petroleum and rubber product. Walt Disney turned to doodling when his cartoons were rejected. His doodles became a little mouse.

My personal coach, Jim Vuocolo, talks about the problems we experience when we work so hard to predetermine and predestine every outcome. "It's like you block off the end of the garden hose," he says. "Try as hard as you can, you can't get that water through. Sometimes we just try so hard to control the outcomes that we block the flow. We work so hard to keep from losing that we can't be free enough to win." The advice Jim shares is to release the outcomes and let things flow. Don't get so bent on things working out a certain way that you miss the opportunities to live creatively along the way.

Don't get so bent on things working out a certain way that you miss the opportunities to live creatively along the way.

Jesus taught that out of death comes new life: *Unless a kernel of wheat falls to the ground and dies, it remains only a single seed. But if it dies, it produces many seeds* (John 12:24). The best place for seed to grow is under the ground; but, the seed will experience death when it gets there. A farmer must be willing to let his seeds get dirty and even die before they can grow into something new. Jesus also taught that there is awesome potential in a seed, *It is like a mustard seed, which a man took and planted in his garden. It grew and became a tree* (Luke 13:19).

It is very possible that out of what seems like a closed door, a failure, or death, will spring the greatest fruitfulness you have experienced yet. You may need to be patient. Always keep looking. The absolute best may be closer than you think.

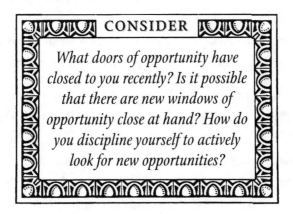

CONSIDER

What doors of opportunity have closed to you recently? Is it possible that there are new windows of opportunity close at hand? How do you discipline yourself to actively look for new opportunities?

20

Instill Purpose in People

*Whatever you do, work at it with all your
heart, as working for the Lord, not for men.*

COLOSSIANS 3:23

Soon Kathy will leave her position as a manager in a major Chicago corporation in order to start her own company. She loves the perks of her job. She enjoys the products she works with and the opportunities she has in her industry. She even likes most of the people she works with, but she's convinced that she can't stay on and maintain her integrity.

She must leave. Her reason: "My company doesn't instill purpose in people. They just treat them like cogs in a wheel. They don't respect them. I hate it." With this disappointment on her mind, Kathy is determined to start a company that does things differently. "I want to lead a company that upholds the value of people," she says. "Respect our suppliers. Treat our employees and our clients with dignity."

William Pollard, long-time chairman of The ServiceMaster Company, believed that this principle impacted the culture and outstanding growth of his company. In his book, *The Soul of the Firm,* he says, "People want to work for a cause, not just a living. When there is alignment between the cause of the firm and the cause of its people, move over—because there will be extraordinary performance."

Paul, too, realized the importance of helping people see purpose in their work. At a time when most laborers worked in sweaty, dirty, and dingy environments, Paul instilled workers with the belief that they could make a difference. He helped them see a bigger purpose. The motivation for their work was more than a paycheck or the potential for promotion. It mattered to *God.* Let's face it, whether we're teachers or tour guides, mechanics or ministers, we all want to know: "Does what I'm doing matter?" "Is this work meaningful?" "Am I doing something that helps humanity or will leave a mark after I'm gone?"

Writing to the Colossian church, Paul taught, *Whatever you do, whether in word or deed, do it all in the name of the Lord Jesus* (Colossians 3:17). His "whatever" included even the items deemed lowly. Addressing slaves and encouraging even them to carry out their work with diligence, he said *Whatever you do, work at it with all your heart, as working for the Lord, not for men* (Colossians 3:23).

When people see their work as part of the bigger picture, they feel motivated to put more into it. Their jobs become a part of self-expression, not just plain old work. They perceive value in what they do and don't need to move up the hierarchy to feel excited about their work. The whole idea of secular work and sacred work dissipates. They see that what they make, the way they serve, the products they sell really can make the world a better place. What a great way to live!

When people see their work as part of the bigger picture, they feel motivated to put more into it.

I asked my friend Sean why he left his lucrative position with an insurance company to take a job with a Midwestern publisher. "Why did you do it?" I asked him.

He thought for a moment, then responded, "Jeff, I realized it meant more to me to work with a group of people on a mission than simply to make more money." And then he said with a smile, "The things we're publishing really do help people."

Today, more companies are harnessing the power of purpose to help workers see the greater value of their work. Ken Blanchard, in his book *Managing by Values,* talks of seeking out "Fortunate 500" companies where both the quality of service available to their customers and the quality of life accessible to their employees are high. "No longer is values-based organizational behavior an interesting philosophical choice—it is a requisite for survival."

Steve Jobs once challenged John Scully, then president of Pepsi-Cola, "Do you want to spend the rest of your life selling sugared water, or do you want a chance to change the world?"[42] Whether or not you agree with Jobs that what Scully was doing was simply peddling "sugared water," you can't argue with his passion to instill a sense of purpose and vision.

"Do you want to spend the rest of your life selling sugared water, or do you want a chance to change the world?"

Core values, where every employee can see his or her role in doing something great together, create a motivating environment for people. "To the extent that the employees in a Fortune 500 organization are truly treated like its most precious resources, they become more committed to its goals than in other organizations where people perceive themselves as being used like expendable commodities."[43]

"We are not machines; we are people, with our own fingerprints of personality and potential," said William Pollard.[44] At the end of the day, we all want to know that our work matters. We want to know that even the most menial, insignificant, or hidden task had value in achieving a worthwhile mission. And like my six-year-old son, we want someone to take a look at what we've done and say, "You did a great job!" "That's great!" "Well done!" We want the creativity, extra hard work, and special touches to be noticed and know they're significant.

What might it mean to strategically instill a sense of purpose in the people around you? What if you help them realize that their work matters and that you noticed it? One female leader I know actually shows It's a Wonderful Life to her team at Christmas, then gathers them around and reads letters to each of them that start, "If you had never been born . . . " You can imagine how her teammates feel about that!

Another leader keeps notes by his desk so that he's regularly reminded to write "thank you" or "well done" to those who stretch or work hard for the goal. "Months later," he says with surprise, "these notes are hanging on walls or on desks." Others just want to know that what they're doing somehow fits into a larger picture—that their part contributes to the achievement of the mission.

If we were to acknowledge to ourselves that our own work matters, might it help us pass such a blessing on to those around us? Perhaps no one has ever done this for you. You've labored unnoticed and unappreciated for much of your career. Could things have been different for you if you had worked in an environment that instilled purpose in people?

"Be bold," said Basil King. "And mighty forces will come to your aid." The bold step you might take today is to simply help one person see that what he or she does has a purpose, and that you notice.

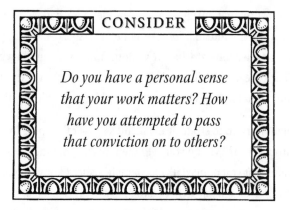

CONSIDER

Do you have a personal sense that your work matters? How have you attempted to pass that conviction on to others?

21

Ask for Help

I, Tertius, who wrote down this letter, greet you in the Lord.

ROMANS 16:22

Interestingly some of Paul's letters were not written by him. Tertius was likely the secretary of Gaius, one of Paul's traveling companions,[45] and he did the actual writing of Paul's letter to the Romans, according to the verse above. Paul spoke. Tertius wrote. Could Paul have done the writing himself? Most likely he could have. He had done it before, but in this instance, Paul accepted help. He asked Tertius to do the writing.

Many entrepreneurial leaders need to grow in their willingness to invite others to participate. There are times that we share our needs with the right people. We let them know there's something that would benefit from their attention. We ask, "Are you available?" At other times, we might bring in subcontractors to do some of the work: temps, designers, programmers, and project managers. We can employ a skilled consultant whose advice could save us valuable time, money, pain, and even the hassle of a costly detour. Sometimes we need to look to other entrepreneurial leaders for guidance or call a special board meeting. But oftentimes, entrepreneurial leaders won't pursue any of these avenues, preferring to do it all themselves.

What usually stands in the way of utilizing these vital resources? As one of my coaching clients recently admitted, "I just hate to ask for help!" Like the Marlboro man in the old cigarette ads, we continue to go it alone. And like the person lost on the highway, we thick headedly refuse to ask for directions.

Like the Marlboro man in the old cigarette ads, we continue to go it alone.

As I write this chapter, I am on a jet somewhere over the North Atlantic having just spent five days with an entrepreneurial leader in the Baltic country of Lithuania. I went to work with this leader because of his willingness to let me know he needed my help. Suffering through the lonely challenges of startup and living in a foreign culture, he reached out and communicated his needs. Instead of being the strong, silent type internalizing his struggles, he sent me an e-mail and shared what he was going through. I couldn't resist responding to his call for help.

Within a few weeks, I boarded a jet and headed to Lithuania to be an encourager, listening ear, consultant, and friend. As I travel home, I feel I have received more than I gave. I had the privilege to share my gifts and play a small role in helping to position him for success. He had my companionship and perspective for just a short time. Not for a moment did I ever consider his request unnecessary or a sign of weakness. On the contrary, I admired his wisdom and willingness to look outside of himself for resources that could help.

It breaks my heart when I hear of leaders who burn out, go under financially, or lose their family or health because they refused to seek help. Help from others offers entrepreneurial leaders counsel, coaching, expertise, and maybe even financial aid. It's okay when you are unable to do everything on your own. There really are others out there who would love to help.

"Why didn't you ask me sooner?" I was asked when I sought assistance to get a mailing out. "I'd love to help!"

"Really?" I said, shocked.

One advisor has told me, "Call me whenever you need me. I don't care if it's in the middle of the night!"

Today, the profession of personal coaching is emerging as entrepreneurial leaders recognize their need for others to come alongside to help. As more people work on their own or start home-based businesses, coaches can be utilized to encourage leaders and help them stay focused on their mission.

Traditionally, the word *coach* has been used in relation to athletics. However, in the fifteenth century, the word referred to a horse-drawn vehicle. The coach would take people from where they were to where they wanted to be.[46] Today more and more leaders hire coaches to help them achieve their best. Like horse-drawn coaches, present-day coaches help entrepreneurial leaders travel from where they are to where they want to be. Whether individuals are in business, a non-profit organization, or just in need of help to reach their goals, they are more likely than ever to seek outside help in the form of a coach.

Leadership guru Warren Bennis said, "Coaching will become the model for leaders in the future. Coaches teach, mentor, and empower.

I am certain that leadership can be learned and that terrific coaches . . . facilitate learning."[47] A good coach won't bring to you talent you don't have, but he or she will help draw to the surface what may be dormant within you. By asking probing questions and helping you clarify your goals and values, coaches bring your best thinking to the forefront. Then they work with you to keep you on track so that you can maximize your potential and achieve your goals.

> A good coach won't bring to you talent you don't have, but he or she will help draw to the surface what may be dormant within you.

A good coach also helps an individual clarify internal and external obstacles and then assists in developing strategies to overcome them. Furthermore, a coach may play a significant role in helping his client to avoid feelings of isolation, which plague so many entrepreneurial leaders. Why endure solitary confinement if you don't have to? For the entrepreneurial leader, a coach may be the best investment you make—an investment in yourself. If you're not thriving, the choice to employ a coach can significantly impact your endeavor.

Few significant missions can be accomplished alone. If you're asking people to volunteer their time, they can always say no if they can't or don't want to become involved. By the same token, if you seek to pay someone for his or her expertise, you can always decide what fee you can afford. You have options.

So, when you become swamped and are in need of help, send up a flare! Let someone know you're in need. Be open to giving someone else a sense of what's on your plate, what you can't do alone. You never know, your endeavor may be the very thing the individual has been looking for!

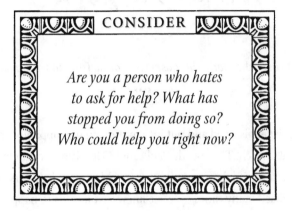

CONSIDER

Are you a person who hates to ask for help? What has stopped you from doing so? Who could help you right now?

22

Share the Vision

All over the world this gospel is bearing fruit and growing.
COLOSSIANS 1:6

Jesus Christ envisioned and put into motion an unstoppable force called the Church. The apostle Paul caught His vision, seeing the Church as a spiritual community that would nurture believers and multiply itself many times over. He knew that for this to happen, it was essential for him to share this vision with others.

Although the Church was just in its infancy, Paul painted a picture of the Gospel bearing fruit and growing *all over the world.* He shared this vision by *admonishing and teaching everyone with all wisdom, so that we may present everyone as perfect in Christ* (Colossians 1:28). Paul envisioned a time when *everyone* would be spiritually mentored, and no one would be left behind. He encouraged the people to imagine that their experience would someday spread to the whole world.

As an example, Paul pointed out to the Colossians that they *learned . . . from Epaphras* (Colossians 1:7). Epaphras was just an ordinary man who passed on to them what he had learned. They in turn were to pass on what they learned. This multiplication process was to continue so that everyone could be presented as perfect in Christ. This vision was so powerful that the Church continues to perpetuate Paul's vision today!

Communicating and sharing the vision is exactly what entrepreneurial leaders do. Like a metaphorical baton, they pass vision from one person to another. They energize people and motivate them to do things they hadn't thought of before. They enlist others in the cause. Passing on the vision may be as simple as asking an individual to give a product a try, but something amazing begins to happen. Like an invisible string of lights coming on inside of people's heads, visions create networks of what Elton Trueblood called "companies of the committed."[48]

Communicating and sharing the vision is exactly what entrepreneurial leaders do. Like a metaphorical baton, they pass vision from one person to another. They energize people and motivate them to do things they hadn't thought of before.

Over the last twelve years, Todd Kurland and his friend, Jacqui have envisioned and started a non-profit organization in Boston called Santa Claus Anonymous, which serves underprivileged children. It is part of what they call their "500-year plan," believing their efforts will continue to impact people that many years from now. They have initiated a winter fund-raising formal called the *Snowball*. The annual event, which is sponsored by major organizations in Boston, currently attracts thousands, raising money for inner-city charities. They also recruit scores of friends to participate in bike-a-thons, walkathons, and even a stair-climbing event in a Boston skyscraper. All of this is part of their 500-year plan!

I have other friends who dream of starting foundations that will fund coaching and consulting for non-profit start-ups. Another envisions a spiritual retreat center in our area as a place for leaders to get away and learn to care for their souls. As I write, this friend is bidding on land a few miles away! Another friend envisions a company that will donate significant amounts of its profits to fund ministry opportunities. These are all visions that these individual have been willing to foster and share.

America's Founding Fathers envisioned a nation "of the people, by the people, and for the people." Henry Ford pictured thousands of factory reproducible and affordable cars. Walt Disney pictured a place in California called Disney Land. Steve Wozniak and Steve Jobs pictured portable computers in people's homes.

Nothing can compare to such powerful idealism and optimism to capture the hearts and imaginations of people and stir them to action. An appealing vision for the future does just that. We need to ask ourselves, *What are we building in the next three to five years? Over the next twenty? In our lifetime? Even the next five hundred?* By definitively answering questions like these, we unleash the imagination and often the creative energy to overcome the great inertia that threatens to stop us before we begin.

"A vision is a mental model of a future state of process, a group, or an organization," says Burt Nanus, author of *Visionary Leadership.* "As such," he continues, "it deals with a world that exists only in the imagination, a world built upon plausible speculations, fabricated from what we hope are reasonable assumptions about the future. . . . A visionary portrays a fictitious world that can be observed or verified in advance. . . . It is a world whose very existence requires an act of faith."[49]

"A visionary portrays a fictitious world that can be observed or verified in advance. . . . It is a world whose very existence requires an act of faith."

While such vision may not come naturally for all entrepreneurial leaders, sharing vision is an invaluable tool for your entrepreneurial arsenal. One team I worked with spent a weekend retreat in a cabin on a lake discussing vision. They were asked where they saw themselves at different stages of the future as well as: "What if we were to take our mission seriously and it was to really work?" "What would be the ripple effects?" As you might imagine, the weekend was filled with energy, and the next months of work were incredibly productive.

You may find it helpful to write a vision statement for your organization. One group of leaders I helped to get started now defines themselves by their vision: The Boston Vision Group. The following statement is repeated at the beginning of every one of their meetings: "Someday Boston will be known as a place where there is infectious Christian community wherever you turn . . . starting with its leaders." And they're seeing it happen.

Even if your vision is clear in your own mind, it may take some work to be able to clearly articulate it so that others get it. You may find it helpful to put yourself through some exercises. Imagine you are ten years in the future. As though you are living then, write a letter to yourself now. Assume the vision you have today has become a reality. What are you doing? What exists that didn't ten years before? What kind of results are you seeing?

One woman I took through this exercise said, "I am now the president of my own company. We are recognized as leaders in our industry, primarily because of our values. We put customers first, value our employees, and make it easy for our customers to do business with us. We now have over a billion dollars in annual revenue and continue to grow our profitability each year."

It's also helpful to create word pictures or analogies to share the vision. A friend of mine who is also a coach describes himself as a miner. He communicates to prospective clients that he mines for the gold inside of individuals and their companies. Another consultant friend speaks of her job as *destagnatizing*. She defines it as helping organizations "get unstuck and create movement when things are stagnant." I often tell her that someday the word *destagnatizing* will be in Webster's Dictionary because of her work. We've even talked about a specific date!

It may take some work to get a truly significant and effective chain reaction started. Inertia takes the most energy when motion is initiated, but long after you are gone, your vision may still be bearing fruit—all over the world.

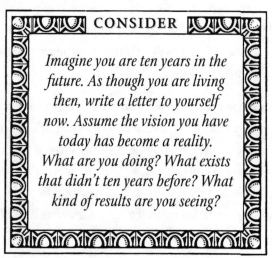

CONSIDER

Imagine you are ten years in the future. As though you are living then, write a letter to yourself now. Assume the vision you have today has become a reality. What are you doing? What exists that didn't ten years before? What kind of results are you seeing?

23

Sow Generously

Whoever sows generously will also reap generously.

2 CORINTHIANS 9:6

We've all wondered at times how much we can afford to give. We check to see how much we have to spare. What will we sacrifice if we give? What will we get in return?

Stephen Covey has made popular a concept he calls "abundance mentality." It's a core belief that there is plenty to go around for everyone, and even more is created when one gives. In direct opposition is what he calls "scarcity mentality," meaning there's only a little bit "out there."[50] According to the abundance mentality, the universe is filled with resources. *I* don't lose just because *you* get something. Or, as a friend of mine taught me, "When the water rises, all the boats rise." Help others get what they want, and you'll receive what you really want.

In his book *The Active Life,* author Parker Palmer shares a related principle. "The quality of our active lives depends heavily on whether we assume a world of scarcity or abundance . . . . In a universe of scarcity, only people who know the arts of competing, even making war, will be able to survive. But in a universe of abundance, acts of generosity and community become not only possible but fruitful as well."[51]

"The quality of our active lives depends
heavily on whether we assume a
world of scarcity or abundance."

Whoever sows generously will also reap generously (2 Corinthians 9:6).
Plant little—grow little. The *Twentieth Century New Testament* version
reads, *scanty sowing, scanty harvest; plentiful sowing, plentiful harvest.*[52]
The image suggests that a sower has a choice whether to give sparingly
or generously. Furthermore, he can predict the end result.

Paul's approach is not the traditional one of guilt but of encouragement—no shoulds or have-tos; no "You're bad if you don'ts." Paul's
teaching on giving is refreshingly positive. He simply explained a principle that is at work in the universe and leaves the decision up to the
individual. He wanted us to see giving as a great opportunity, as enjoyable and rewarding, instead of a requirement, forcing individuals to
surrender their stuff. *Each man should give what he has decided in his
heart to give, not reluctantly or under compulsion, for God loves a cheerful
giver* (2 Corinthians 9:7).

Author and leadership teacher John Haggai wrote in his book *Lead On*
that giving generates more giving. We bless and are blessed. We grace
and are graced. He writes, "What do you want? Sow it. Invest it. Do you
want friends? Invest friendship. Do you want love? Invest love. Do you
want respect? Invest respect. Those who are excellent leaders reflect this
passion to give rather than to take. . . . The takers ultimately lose."[53]

As I watch the friends I went to college with grow older, I begin to
notice a trend. Those who seem to accumulate wealth in healthy ways
lead rich and happy lives, and they're generous—sometimes incredibly

generous. They open their homes to others and help the poor. They serve on boards of organizations they care about, and they give money to their churches and favorite charities. Some of them are even involved with the poor and underprivileged on a personal basis—and their net worth continues to grow in every way.

One friend gave away an old car he was no longer using to a person in need. Another classmate paid for an individual to attend a leadership retreat. Still another friend who owns an automobile franchise donates cars to be used by his church. Another of my classmates lives in Europe and is starting a small group in her home to mentor struggling mothers. I believe these generous friends have a healthy view of money. It doesn't own or control them, and they use it as a tool to bless others.

The Bible is quite clear about the spiritual principle of sowing and reaping. Those who give freely will receive in one way or another. They create positive space for more when other items are cleared out. Like cleaning out a cluttered closet, they make room for new things. They free space in their hearts and open up themselves for growth. Hearts that hoard and grasp just become stuffed. They stifle new growth.

Jesus taught, *It is more blessed to give than to receive* (Acts 20:35). Obviously, this is not the fast track to instant wealth. The moment I give, I have quantitatively less. Still, these words speak to our hearts that to give is a great blessing. When we give, our hearts swell, and we're able to accept more. We create space in our lives, and somehow I think God must say, "Okay, you're ready for Me to entrust you with more. I know you're not going to hoard it."

One of my coaching clients questioned, "But can this principle work in a dog-eat-dog business world? I work with some pretty fierce people. Some of them would be glad to see me out of business!"

"It all depends," I said. "Do we want short-term or long-term gain? Though it's not always easy to see with the physical eye, I believe that those who give will receive—and with a large amount of interest."

The last time I had my hair cut, I was mistakenly charged twice. When I explained the situation, not only did the manager humbly apologize and refund my money—she offered to give me that haircut free. Instead of questioning my situation, she believed me and demonstrated generosity. In doing so, she kept me as a client.

Every once in a while, it's good to take an inventory of what we've accumulated to discover what we need to give away. We need to make room in our closets, our wallets, our hearts, and even our calendars. What seeds do we need to sow? What gifts do we need to give? What need are we in the best position to meet?

Every once in a while, it's good to take an inventory of what we've accumulated to discover what we need to give away. We need to make room in our closets, our wallets, our hearts, and even our calendars.

This will require continual faith, but as hockey great Wayne Gretzky said, "You miss 100 percent of the shots you never take." Maybe this is the time for you to stretch yourself in the area of giving. In the natural sense, you will take a risk; however, the One with whom you will be taking this risk is utterly trustworthy. As you take the step to give, the miracle of new growth will occur—even if you don't see it immediately.

In return you will receive a gift of inner freedom. As songwriter Michael Card sings, "We can't imagine the freedom we find from the things we leave behind."[54] Paul might then add, "and give away."

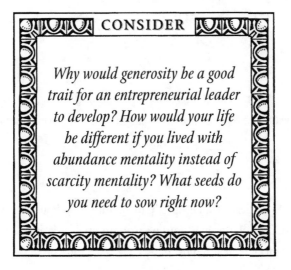

CONSIDER

Why would generosity be a good trait for an entrepreneurial leader to develop? How would your life be different if you lived with abundance mentality instead of scarcity mentality? What seeds do you need to sow right now?

24

Find Good in Adversity

We know that all things work together for good to them that
love God, to them who are the called according to his purpose.

ROMANS 8:28 KJV

Have you ever been in a situation that seemed so horrid that you said, or at least wondered things like: "Can anything good possibly come from this?" No matter how hard we work to prevent it, life gets messy. Circumstances arise and most of us say, "What did I do to deserve this? This isn't what I bargained for."

From a rat-infested prison cell, Paul somehow saw the bright side in the midst of his adversity. He didn't see the prison as the end of the line. Instead, he claimed that he was actually *an ambassador in chains* (Ephesians 6:20).

That is an interesting choice of words. Webster's Dictionary defines an *ambassador* as a "messenger or authorized envoy; an official representative." *Chains* are described as "that which binds, restrains, or confines." The two words together sound more like an oxymoron—a *confined envoy*. What a contrast. But Paul refused to describe his chains as a hindrance. He wrote, *It has become clear throughout the*

whole palace guard and to everyone else that I am in chains for Christ
(Philippians 1:13).

There's no doubt that Paul suffered for his cause, but he knew he had
the freedom to choose how he responded. As author John Ortberg
writes, "Suffering always changes us, but not always for the better."[55]
This was not the case with Paul, nor should it be with us. Most of us
don't include suffering as part of our strategic growth plan, but we can
always use it to our advantage.

Most of us don't include suffering as part
of our strategic growth plan, but we
can always use it to our advantage.

Unfortunately, most of us seem to avoid harsh training. It reminds me
of a book title: *Pain: the Gift No One Wants.*[56] When we wake up on the
cold prison floors of our own adversity, we have the opportunity to see
promise in the pain. Do you see the potential? Does that image make
you want to respond by saying, "Oh boy! Sign me up!" Probably not,
but it is possible for us to turn bleak situations into creative ones. We
can make lemonade from lemons!

Paul wasn't a complainer either. He recognized his difficult situation
contained an element of the greater good. As he wrote to the church in
Rome, *We know that in all things God works for the good of those who love
him* (Romans 8:28). Perhaps it was in the midst of his own adversity
that he learned the lesson he taught us in Romans: *Suffering produces
perseverance; perseverance, character; and character, hope* (Romans 5:3-4).

As difficult as it seems, Paul didn't see his captors as his adversaries. Instead, they became his captive audience. They were stuck listening to his pitch. The dungeon also provided an opportunity to do some direct marketing with the Roman military. Paul realized his chains could bring attention to his message when people questioned, "Why is this man thought to be so dangerous? What is Rome trying to keep us from hearing? Might there be something to this message?"

My wife, Mindy, and her friend Kari have coined a new term for such unsuspected opportunities—they call it "Scenario Q." When our Scenarios A, B, and C aren't working out, God just may be getting ready to bring about "Scenario Q." It's not part of *our* original strategic plan, but we can view it as an unforeseen opportunity—a hidden pearl created by a little piece of sand stuck in an oyster.

Perhaps Scenario Q is the product that no one else cared about, the opportunity we neglected, or the person we failed to see as a source of wisdom. In Paul's case, he was a man in chains, locked up in a dungeon, who recognized the opportunity to influence the world with his mission. Most simply abandoned him. They wrote him off as a failed leader. Yet, as Samuel Rima writes, "It is doubtful that there is a single person alive today who has not in some way been affected by this self-employed tent maker."[57]

The truth is that most of us can't, or won't, see such hidden potential. It's been said that only 3 percent of people jump into an idea right up front. The next 10 percent will invest after some careful examination. The next 10 percent after they've seen a prototype. Most simply don't recognize an opportunity when they see it. It's a matter of perspective. Thomas Edison invented the light bulb only after experiencing many dead ends and seeming failures. "I know a thousand ways how not to

FIND GOOD IN ADVERSITY

make a light bulb," he said. Similarly, Winston Churchill said, "Success is going from failure to failure without losing enthusiasm."

Craig Hall, chairman of Hall Financial Group, wrote, "In my career, I have often done things others perceived to be very risky. Many of the properties my company bought were in terrible physical and financial condition and often were in default on debts. But I saw opportunity when others only saw problems."[58]

I realize this comes easier for some than others. Some people seem to hop out of bed each day with a smile and a can-do attitude. They don't bother reading self-help and faith-inspiring books because they don't need them. "I'm just pretty happy-go-lucky," said my friend who runs a profitable car dealership. "I don't quite understand why others struggle so much to see the bright side." But I think people this optimistic are in the minority.

For the rest of us, it's part of our life's job description to intentionally search for the ray of hope when our world grows dark and dreary. Effort is required. Whether it's self-help books, walks in the woods, fishing trips, massages, or mentoring from positive people, most of us need help! It's up to us to find solutions. No one else can do it for us.

It's part of our life's job description to intentionally search for the ray of hope when our world grows dark and dreary.

It would be easy to blame the challenges and obstacles on bad luck, lack of training, inadequate intellect, bad market conditions, a needy spouse, or lack of capital. However, like Paul, we need to shift our perspective to seek possibility in adversity. We will have to fight the darkness in our own souls and develop the muscle of our faith. We need to see every situation as one that can be used for good.

History tells us that the message of Christianity spread throughout the world by means of the Roman soldiers who caught the message of faith. Although Paul was in chains, his message wasn't, and God used it to change the world.

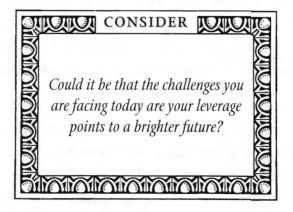

CONSIDER

Could it be that the challenges you are facing today are your leverage points to a brighter future?

25

Define the Mission

*To call people from among all the Gentiles
to the obedience that comes from faith.*

ROMANS 1:5

When I played quarterback on my high school football team, I experienced some pretty bleak games marked by interceptions and fumbles. My teammates (thinking they were funny) created their own version to the song Diana Ross made popular, "Do You Know Where You're Going To?" Imagine walking into a packed high school lunchroom on a Monday and being greeted by a bunch of hulking linemen singing, "Do you know who you're throwing to? Don't you like the blocks your line was throwing you? Who were you throwing to? Do you know?" Unfortunately, I knew they were right! I hadn't seen my receivers too clearly that weekend.

Those who connect with you regarding your mission need to know, "Do you know where you're going to?" They need to know where you're headed, how you plan to get there, and why you are doing it. Few will fully commit unless they know. Like one preacher said, "When there's a mist in the pulpit, there's a fog in the pew!" If what we're doing is the slightest bit unclear in our minds, it will be very fuzzy for others. Proverbs speaks to this need for clarity: *Where there is no vision, the people perish* (Proverbs 29:18 KJV).

In her book, *The Path,* Laurie Beth Jones speaks to this issue. "Knowing your personal mission statement is the best career insurance you can have, because once you are clear about what you were put here to do, then 'jobs' become only a means toward your mission, not an end in themselves." For the organization, this becomes even more significant. "Governments as well as companies and individuals are struggling almost daily to define their specific area of responsibility. There is a need for clarity, for language that creates the boundaries of what we're doing and not doing."[59]

"Knowing your personal mission statement
is the best career insurance you can have,
because once you are clear about what you were
put here to do, then 'jobs' become only a means
toward your mission, not an end in themselves."

Paul was able to clearly define, articulate, and present what he was called to do and often did so at the beginnings of his letters. "I'm Paul, and my mission is *to call people from among all the Gentiles [non-Jewish people] to the obedience that comes from faith* (Romans 1:5). His three-part mission statement can serve as a template for our own statements.

First, Paul was actively engaged in activity—his *calling,* his *mission.* Paul was a communicator, and this was his way of proclaiming and inviting.

Second, the *target* audience of Paul's activity was the Gentiles. Third, the *outcome* Paul sought to achieve was for the Gentiles to become obedient through faith, resulting in transformed lives. The following is my mission statement: "Unlocking visionary people to turn their dreams into reality." The activity is *unlocking*. The target audience is *visionary people*. The outcome is that *they turn their dreams into reality*. Writing this book is consistent with my mission statement.

Of course, there are many resources to assist you in crafting your mission statement, but you can spare yourself a lot of expense by simply applying Paul's technique. The key is to define the inner reality. Your mission statement will most likely be discovered, not concocted. It already exists in your desires or in the activity already taking place. All you need to do is put it into words that create the boundaries and definitions to articulate the mission clearly.

Start by asking what action you or your organization is pursuing. For example, are you communicating, serving, building, helping, establishing, inventing, creating, or giving? Usually your action stirs you or it represents something that you do best. You probably love doing it, and even thinking about it creates a certain amount of enthusiasm. It's your passion.

Next, who or what is your target audience? For Paul, it was specifically the Gentiles. For you, it may be a group of people such as leaders, men, professionals, small business owners, inner-city children, people in Miami, lawyers, or mothers. It may be a project such as welfare reform, urban housing, excellent dairy products, quality recreational events, or reasonably priced health care.

Finally, what do you hope to accomplish through your action? This answers the question, "What do I want the outcome to be?" It might be to provide a way for others to experience a healthier lifestyle, a higher standard of living, authentic spirituality, or higher profits for you and your investors.

Once you define it, go public with your mission. Tell others. Paul chose the beginning of his letters as the vehicle to do this. Kelly Insurance Company in Maryland has emblazoned its mission statement in a prominent spot in its lobby and in its published material. One cannot miss that they value and serve their suppliers and their customers and seek to honor God in the way they do business.

Gourmet Ice Cream makers, Ben & Jerry's, divide their mission into three parts: a product mission, a social mission, and an economic mission. Each is inscribed on the walls of its factories. It is a public statement meant for internal and external consumption. Another example is Tom's of Maine, which makes all-natural toothpaste and other personal products. They teach a curriculum quarterly so that all associates will have a thorough understanding of the company's mission.

Your mission statement will be the lifeblood of your endeavor. It will galvanize others who will resonate and willingly participate, often for reasons beyond financial gain. They may simply want to be a part of something meaningful that will make the world a better place.

Your mission statement will be the lifeblood of your endeavor. It will galvanize others who will resonate and willingly participate.

With his mission firmly established, Paul remained resolute and able to overcome impediments: *hardships and distresses; . . . beatings,*

imprisonments and riots . . . hard work, sleepless nights and hunger (2
Corinthians 6:4-5). To the elders of the church at Ephesus he wrote,
*You know that I have not hesitated to preach anything that would be
helpful to you but have taught publicly and from house to house* (Acts
20:20). Paul was determined to accomplish his mission, so much so
that near the end of his life, he was able to write with confidence, *I
have fought the good fight, I have finished the race, I have kept the faith*
(2 Timothy 4:7).

If you haven't done so already, you can create a mission statement that
will serve as a beacon to all who read it. Find it. Define it. Unleash it,
and let it guide you to the results you desire.

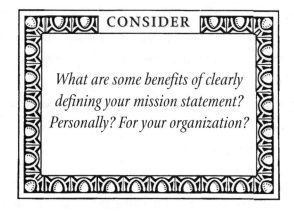

CONSIDER

*What are some benefits of clearly
defining your mission statement?
Personally? For your organization?*

26

Let Go of Your No's

Some of them sneered, but others said,
"We want to hear you again on this."
ACTS 17:32

Have you ever been *sneered* at? The word itself sounds like it feels. *Sneeeerrrr.* It means "to show contempt by a particular facial expression." I remember childhood experiences with my now much-reformed older brother. "You what?" he'd say with a raised eyebrow and scrunched mouth. It certainly didn't sit well in this little kid's brain. I can still picture his face and feel the depression that came over me as if it were just yesterday.

Paul knew what it was like to be jeered by the very people he was trying to help. To the majority of the Athenians, Paul's talk about the resurrection of the dead was both outrageous and ridiculous. It was comical. The very idea that the apostle believed a man could actually return from the dead seemed absurd. Some responded with outright scorn. Others listened politely but weren't convinced. Still others suggested that they might be open to hearing him speak more on the subject at a later date. In other words, they took a "we'll see" attitude.

Unfortunately, most entrepreneurial leaders will face sneers, "no ways," and polite no's. You most likely know what I'm talking about: the "no" from the investor, the "no" from the potential client, the "no" from what was thought to be a sure sale, and even a "no" from the government. At one point, Paul and Barnabus *shook the dust from their feet* (Acts 13:51), symbolically saying, "We won't have anything to do with you anymore." Today, we simply wash our hands and no longer communicate with the person. We take our marbles and go elsewhere!

You can imagine how people responded when Christopher Columbus proposed that the earth was round: "No way!" Abraham Lincoln received his share of no's when he repeatedly ran for public office and lost. Then there was Thomas Edison who said he had discovered countless ways *not* to invent a light bulb. But although we're in good company, it is still tough for most of us to hear the word *no*. We don't like the feeling of being rejected or being picked last or passed over altogether. We'd rather not hear "no thanks" or "I'll pass" from those who don't buy into our ideas. No matter how many times we get a yes, we will still have to deal with no's.

No matter how many times we get a yes,
we will still have to deal with no's.

In the midst of raising money for a non-profit organization, a wise person reminded me, "Remember, Jeff, when a foundation or a person says no, they're not rejecting you personally. They're just saying no to the opportunity. It may not be the right one for them, or the timing could be wrong." Another person encouraged, "See your no's as a sign that people are at least giving you the time of day. They know you're asking them something, and at least they listened."

Can you believe that your no's are seldom personal? In most cases the individuals who say no won't think it's a personal issue at all. It is possible that they didn't quite understand what you had to offer. Maybe you're even better off without their participation! It's time to stop worrying and wondering and move on. Think of it like one salesman does. He becomes excited about the fact that with every no he hears, he's statistically that much closer to a yes! If you hear a no, just pick yourself up, dust yourself off, and go on to the next person.

Paul demonstrated a relentlessness and dogged willingness to keep scattering seed, and he let go of the results. Jesus taught that when seeds are sown, some inevitably fall along the path and are eaten by birds. Some fall on rocky ground that has no soil and are eventually scorched by the sun. Some fall among the thorns and are choked out by weeds. But some of the seed fall on good soil and produce a crop that is thirty, sixty, or a hundred times what was sown (Matthew 13:1-9).

Your job is often to just keep asking. Keep asking for the order. Keep seeking the investment and inviting others to participate. Each time you ask, the possibility arises that you'll hear a no; but you'll eventually get a yes. You must continue to let go of all your no's and keep moving forward.

Your job is often to just keep asking. Keep asking for the order. Keep seeking the investment and inviting others to participate. Each time you ask, the possibility arises that you'll hear a no; but you'll eventually get a yes.

Your willingness to trust God with the outcome will bear great dividends in you and through you. Sure, some will say no, but eventually you will find, as Paul did, that some will listen. Some will say yes. *A few men became followers of Paul and believed* (Acts 17:34). The long-term gain was worth the short-term pain.

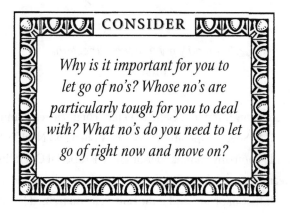

CONSIDER

Why is it important for you to let go of no's? Whose no's are particularly tough for you to deal with? What no's do you need to let go of right now and move on?

27

Help Them Up

To Timothy my true son in the faith.

1 TIMOTHY 1:2

In a *Fast Company* interview, General Peter Scheumacher, commander in chief of U.S. Special Operations, told Eli Cohen and Noel Tichy, "If you're a rifle-company commander or an SOF (Special Operations Forces) team commander, you may well be the casualty of the first bullet. . . . If that happens, and if the unit that you trained has the discipline and the character to accomplish its objective without you, then that's a reflection of your commitment and your contribution."[60]

The principle described by Scheumacher might be called "Help Them Up." In other words, teach them to do your job—duplicate yourself. That's exactly what Paul taught and modeled. He refused to see people as passive parishioners sentenced to inhabit a pew. Instead, he brought them into leadership. He saw potential and actualized it. He wrote to his protégé Timothy, *The things you have heard me say in the presence of many witnesses entrust to reliable men who will also be qualified to teach others* (2 Timothy 2:2). To the Galatian church, Paul spoke of his own agony of waiting until *Christ is formed* in them (Galatians 4:19). Paul's goal was certainly not to remain an all-knowing one-man show. It was to give others opportunities to grow. He encouraged Titus to *Appoint elders in every town* (Titus 1:5). He urged older women to *train the younger women* (Titus 2:4).

In the interview, General Scheumacher said, "Everybody's got to know how to be a leader. They must be able to martial 'creative solutions' in ambiguous circumstances."[61] How willing are you to create that kind of leadership culture? To form an environment where others' strengths are cultivated and can flourish? It could mean that you even hire or empower people who are more proficient in an area than you. Would you give them the floor to speak while you sit quietly and take notes? Would you allow them to receive recognition from media or management, or would you feel threatened and seek to squelch them? Could you humbly allow others to do what they do best?

How willing are you to create that kind of leadership culture? To form an environment where others' strengths are cultivated and can flourish?

It's clear that Paul was a genius when it came to people development. He met people with a hint of potential and invited them into a process of growth. He believed that even the most raw recruit could engage in a process of spiritual formation and leadership training. His goal was more than persuading people to accept the message. It was for their complete transformation and the establishment of an ever-expanding team of leaders.

Entrepreneurial leaders have the opportunity to make use of vast resources of untapped people potential. As was mentioned earlier, most people only utilize about 10 percent of their potential. Inside the human brain lie vast caverns of untouched capacity for growth and activity. What might happen if more people envisioned what they could become and took steps toward becoming their truest selves? What if we as entrepreneurial leaders saw part of our job description as being to release these vast untapped resources in people, to help them be all they can be?

A female leader of a large Cambridge software company told me that one of her major goals is to give those she manages experience and exposure. "When they get major opportunities, I'm their biggest fan," she says. "I want to see them fly."

Those of us who have experience in leadership positions may need to admit that a significant bottleneck to dynamic growth might be due to our unwillingness to follow this principle. We've allowed our own pride and fear of being shown up to keep us from developing the other leaders around us. We haven't brought them along. We've held on to responsibilities that others would gladly share if we would let them. We've tried to be expert know-it-alls instead of developing a team to which we could delegate, allowing the organization to run more efficiently. The truth is that if we will loosen our grip, it will free us up to develop yet untapped resources in ourselves.

Fortunately, many today are recognizing this error and are bringing about change. In the Church, many are rediscovering the idea of gift-based ministry—of equipping all to fulfill each person's purpose. A "new reformation" is emerging, including a conviction that church leaders *prepare God's people for works of service* (Ephesians 4:12). Leaders are learning to give influence away; to allow those with gifts of leadership to lead; those with gifts of teaching to teach; those with gifts of service to serve. Leaders are encouraging people to surpass them. And they're learning to create an environment where it's okay to get your hands dirty, make mistakes, and find new opportunities. As Cohen and Tichy write, "In the SOF, heroes are teachers."[62]

Leaders are encouraging people to surpass them.

We can't call everyone to the same place. We don't ask people to do things that aren't inside them in any way, shape, or form. Instead, the entrepreneurial leader watches people and studies what they do well and what they don't do so well. It's also insightful to understand what people have done in the past and what they have accomplished. Ask them what accomplishments they are most proud of, even as far back as their childhoods. Then listen to hear the patterns of motivation. See what excites them and seek to provide opportunities that engage them in similar ways.

What could happen if we were brave enough to become students of our protégés in the areas they are strongest? What if we were to seek out those with latent leadership and help them envision a future where they are the point men? What if we were to give away the best opportunities? Do you envision these kinds of things for those in your employ?

In the short term, this type of growth may feel unnerving. You will be taking a risk, but in the long run, we can't lose—everyone wins.

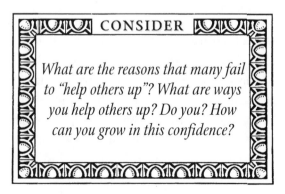

CONSIDER

What are the reasons that many fail to "help others up"? What are ways you help others up? Do you? How can you grow in this confidence?

28

Clarify What's Important

*The important thing is that in every way, whether
from false motives or true, Christ is preached.*

PHILIPPIANS 1:18

Although Paul was continually barraged with divergent agendas and
belief systems, he knew how to answer the question, "What's most
important?" For him it was that *Christ is preached.* His overarching
conviction was that his other tasks paled in comparison. His mission
was more important than hounding those with faulty methods and
wrong ambitions, more important than convincing others to obey religious rules and regulations. By clarifying what was most important, he
knew what to do and what *not* to do. Sometimes the latter is even more
valuable than the former. Have you asked yourself recently, "What
things will I *not* do today?"

Each day you and I are given the gift of 86,400 seconds of time to use
however we see fit. We can't carry any of them over to the next day or
elongate them in any way. None of us has any more or less. Time often
seems harsh and unstoppable, especially when we have so many things
we *could* do. Theologian Dorothy Bass says that for many of us, "Time
continues to be a source not only of pressure but also of guilt and judg-
ment. . . . We delude ourselves into believing that if we can just get

everything done, if we can only tie up all the loose ends, if we can even once get ahead of the crush, we will prove our worth and establish ourselves in safety."[63]

Stephen Covey in his book *Principle Centered Leadership* entitles a chapter "The Main Thing Is to Keep the Main Thing the Main Thing."[64] In other words, don't lose the forest for the trees. Stay on course. Do what matters most. Paul certainly would have agreed.

For many of us, keeping the main thing the main thing presents a significant dilemma. What is the main thing? Knowing that isn't always easy, especially if you're your own boss and don't have a superior to dictate the priorities. It's often helpful to ask ourselves, What is the main thing? What is it for this company? What is it for me? What's the main thing this week? What's the main thing today? We know that interruptions and other items on our agendas will barge in to distract us. We must learn to focus on what matters most.

We must learn to focus on what matters most.

Talaine Medeirer's book on coaching principles has introduced me to the habit of asking three very helpful questions:

- What's most important today?
- What must get done today?
- What's important for the future?[65]

Try writing these questions in a journal or day planner, then answer them. Do this daily if possible. Try it for a week. Some days you'll discover that what's most important is your health. Another day rest will top the list. Other days your marriage, time with family, service opportunities, or spiritual growth may be the highest priority. Perhaps you need time with a key teammate. Other times certain projects will clearly emerge as top on the list.

Personally, when I start my day with these questions, then review them at night, I relax. I'm calmer, and I exhibit greater focus—ultimately I'm more productive. I don't sweat the small stuff. In fact, it's easier now for me to recognize those things that fall into that category. Then I act on what I really want and need to do. I love what Hyrum Smith said in his book, *Ten Natural Laws of Successful Time and Life Management.* "This simple concept of making sure that our daily activities reflect our deepest core values, is the concept that has made all the difference in my own life."[66]

This process of determining what is most important can also help define the values for your organization or enterprise. Ask yourself, "What's most important for our organization? What must we get done? What's most important for our future?" Then write down the answer to each and visibly post them somewhere. Asking these questions may be a great way to start a new year or provide the focus of a leadership retreat.

"Time is neutral;" said Winston Churchill, "but it can be made the ally of those who will seize it and use it to the full." This ability to seize time likely starts when you determine what "to the full" means to you. Once that is clarified, commit to what you value most. I think it's safe to say that no one on their deathbed ever regretfully declares, "Darn, I did too many really important things."

"Time is neutral;" said Winston Churchill,
"but it can be made the ally of those
who will seize it and use it to the full."

Seize your day and make that time work for you instead of you working for it.

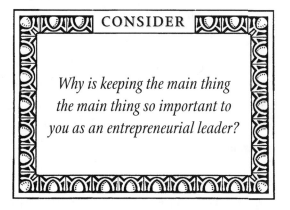

CONSIDER

Why is keeping the main thing the main thing so important to you as an entrepreneurial leader?

29

Team With Others

*Paul and Barnabus remained in Antioch, where they and
many others taught and preached the word of the Lord.*

ACTS 15:35

We've all gone into relationships with the best of intentions only to
later experience conflict in the chemistry, vision, or values. People
problems can be our most troubling and taxing—emotionally, spiritually, and professionally.

"Ah—relationships—they're so *hard!*" says my friend Tom. Another
friend, John shares, "I sometimes dream of riding a Harley [motorcy-
cle] solo across the country," just so he can escape some of the people
challenges for a few hours. Then there's the billboard outside of down-
town Boston advertising iced-tea. The name of the company follows
the words "A Family Business Since 1976" and in small print at the
bottom "Yes, we're presently in counseling."

Working with people can become complicated because each of us
brings to the table our individual personalities, ways of viewing the
world, different backgrounds, and ways of doing things. It's no wonder
there are times when we don't get along.

Paul was no stranger to the turbulent waters of partnerships. He experienced conflict with Peter over doctrinal issues; a *sharp disagreement* with Barnabus that caused them to part company (Acts 15:39); and a deep wound from a man named Alexander, who Paul says, *did me a great deal of harm* (2 Timothy 4:14).

As difficult as people can be, however, the rewards of teaming with others can far surpass the liabilities. In spite of Paul's negative experiences, he still co-labored with apostles, leaders, and preachers. He counted on these partners to share the burdens, the joys, and the opportunities. He practiced synergy—doing more together than individuals can do apart—long before it was defined as an "effective habit."[67]

Paul aligned himself with Barnabus, then Silas, and with *the apostles and elders* when key beliefs needed to be defined (Acts 15:22). Later, he worked closely with Timothy, and made tents with Aquila and Priscilla (Acts 18:1-4). In Antioch he worked with *many others* who *taught and preached the word of the Lord* (Acts 15:35). All of these people were similar to Paul in mission and values, yet very different in gifts and temperaments.

Some entrepreneurial leaders find it valuable to create short-term or project-related teams. Others may contribute to an enterprise by being part of a research and development team, collaborating on the design of a particular project. It's surprising how much input people are willing to contribute free of charge because they're interested in what the other party is doing. The next time you are working on a project, invite anyone expressing an interest to be a part of a short-term team, and just see what happens.

Perhaps it would be helpful to partner with complimentary or related services. They cooperate for a specific amount of time or until certain results have been achieved. Perhaps they can offer credibility or expand your sphere of influence. If you're a small or one-person start-up, such a strategic alliance is invaluable and offers the relational support you're looking for.

Some people do better in partnership arrangements than others. It is helpful to do what works best for you. Look at your past for clues. When you were in the fourth grade, how did you relate to your peers? Did you have a buddy? Did you hang around with a group of close friends or were you a loner? Were you always the leader or often a follower?

The best collaborative partnerships are usually not with people who are just like us but who bring different skills and attributes to the table. They may share the same mission or vision, but possess different strengths and abilities. One person is great at organizing, details, and finances, while another is proficient at casting vision and selling. One person loves to design and develop products, and another prefers to run the business and get it into the marketplace.

The best collaborative partnerships are usually not with people who are just like us but who bring different skills and attributes to the table.

Collaborative relationships are everywhere. Some I am personally familiar with are Ben and Jerry, of ice cream fame; and in the Boston area, Barry and Eliot of Kaufmanns Furniture. My good friends Vance and Steve are successful collaborators for Foundation of the Heart.

Partnering and sub-contracting with other specialists is a growing trend. Next time you're in an airport, notice the names of the various shops and vendors: Ben & Jerry's, Bath and Body Works, Seattle's Best, Cinnabon, and Au Bon Pain. No more bad airport food or junky gift shops. The people who run airports have realized that they need to stick with running airports and let those with the expertise make the coffee and sticky buns. The result is an enjoyable atmosphere where travelers can spend their time between flights. What a great example of synergy in action!

Many are even starting to see sales as a way to team up. *Stop Selling, Start Partnering,* reads the title of Larry Wilson's book.[68] Wilson's thesis is that instead of seeing your job as "getting others to buy," see your specialty as complimenting theirs. Ask how you can help them do what they do best. Create valuable products or services to meet real needs of others.

The biblical principle is clear. *Two are better than one, because they have a good return for their work; if one falls down, his friend can help him up. But pity the man who falls and has no one to help him up! . . . A cord of three strands is not quickly broken* (Ecclesiastes 4:9-10, 12).

You don't need to do it all or even know how to do it all. Learn ways to understand one another. When conflicts arise, and they do, work through your differences. Form covenants that lay out your expectations. Build partnerships of trust in which mutual parties win. You don't want to enter into partnerships with just anyone. Be wise in your selection of partners, but then team up and enjoy the ride.

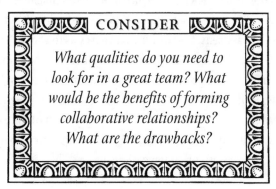

CONSIDER

What qualities do you need to look for in a great team? What would be the benefits of forming collaborative relationships? What are the drawbacks?

30

Do Whatever It Takes

I do all this for the sake of the gospel, that I may share in its blessings.

1 CORINTHIANS 9:23

Throughout history people have regarded Paul as many things: fanatic, zealot, male chauvinist, and diehard. Certainly, no one accused Paul of being lukewarm, halfhearted, or indifferent. He sold out to his calling, his message, and his church community; he doggedly followed God. He was hungry. Once committed, he refused to look back. Today the impact of Paul's resolution reverberates around the world. *For to me, to live is Christ and to die is gain,* he said (Philippians 1:21). And *I have become all things to all men so that by all possible means I might save some. I do all this for the sake of the gospel* (1 Corinthians 9:22-23).

Cervantes observed, "There's no sauce in the world like hunger." Hunger is that uneasy sensation that craves satisfaction. It's deep desire—an uneasy sensation inside that rouses us to action. Sometimes it's a divine dissatisfaction with what is. Other times it's a desire for more of what could be. Paul wanted more. He was driven to excellence for the glory of God. If there's one thing that all entrepreneurial leaders have in common, it's the hungry heart of the explorer. It's a fierce desire to at least try. Zealousness led Paul to embark on missionary journey after missionary journey.

"There's no sauce in the world like hunger."

That same zealousness in 1914, led Ernest Shackleton to set out for Antarctica. He bought a boat called the *Endurance* and placed an ad in a London newspaper through which he recruited twenty-seven men to join him in his quest. They willingly jeopardized their health, their safety, their sanity, and their lives in a quest to find an overland route to the South Pole. When the ice violently crushed and destroyed their boat, they painstakingly fought overwhelming odds to trek their way back to safety. That same commitment led Louis and Clark to set out to map the West and make their way to the Pacific. It beckoned Amelia Earhardt to fly around the world.

So, what's worthy of that kind of investment or commitment? For many people today, not much! To paraphrase Thoreau, "Most people live lives of quiet desperation." Many live with endless boredom. Certainly, none of us wants to sell out to a dead-end crusade. But we also don't want to rust out and waste our lives puttering around. In some reflective moments, we ask, "What really makes me want to 'go for it'? What's worth me giving my all? What deserves my best efforts?"

What would you do if you could do anything and you knew you couldn't fail? That's what we need to decide. No one can decide that for us. What will you do, and what will you not do? Frankly, I love adventure, but I would never have joined Shackleton on that voyage to the South Pole in subzero temperatures and darkness for much of the year. I've already lived in Ithaca, New York, long enough to know that's not for me. To help people connect authentically to God and to each other in community, to help people understand and engage their calling, to coach entrepreneurial leaders to help them succeed, *that* I can do all day!

What would you do if you could do anything and you knew you couldn't fail?

What are you committed to and who else is committed to that? Who might be committed if you invited them?

"One of the best things in my life right now is partnering with some guys who would take a bullet for me," says Vance Brown, cofounder of Foundation of the Heart.

His teammate Matt agrees, "That's why I left my job to help these guys. They're really committed to this—and they're committed to me. I've never been a part of anything like this before."

My friend and mentor Jim Frost shares that the camaraderie he experienced as a soldier during the Vietnam War was often what kept him going. "In many ways you fought for your buddies," he told me. "You'd do anything for them, and they'd do anything for you. You knew these guys were in it with you." Jim's job was to walk "point" through the jungles. "Yes, I was kind of crazy," he says. "The life expectancy of a point man once combat began was less than half a second. But somehow . . . God brought me back alive!"

What's worth holding out for? Fighting for? Working your tail off for? We need to revisit those questions periodically. Once we have our answers, what are we willing to give up to do it? Safety? Financial security? The approval of others? Time and energy?

Paul was our example. He was willing to do whatever it took.

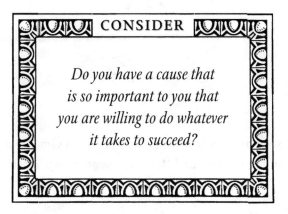

CONSIDER

*Do you have a cause that
is so important to you that
you are willing to do whatever
it takes to succeed?*

31

Serve Them

*Serve one another in love. The entire law is summed up
in a single command: "Love your neighbor as yourself."*

GALATIANS 5:13-14

I met with a counselor a few years ago to address anxiety issues. I continually woke up at 2:30 in the morning unable to get back to sleep. As I lay in bed, my mind whirled with conversations, problems, and to-do lists. The more I tried to erase them from my mind, the more I worried. In retrospect, I realize that I was struggling with borderline depression as well. The combination adversely affected my marriage, my health, and my ability to function during the day. Let's just say, it wasn't a fun season.

"What are you trying so hard to *do* Jeff?" my counselor asked me.

"What do you mean?" I said.

"What are you trying to accomplish? What's so important that it's costing you your sleep?"

I thought for a moment then said, "I think I'm just trying to succeed," I said. "I want to figure out how to get it all done. I lie in bed thinking about it all night. I feel trapped by my own run-away brain."

"Is it helpful?" he asked.

"What? Obsessing about all this? No!" I said, kind of upset. "I end up making bad choices—I hurt people. It's not like I'm trying to, though."

"Let me make a suggestion," he finally proposed. "You seem to be asking yourself an unhelpful question. You're basically asking yourself, 'How can I succeed today?' Instead, what if you were to ask, 'How can I serve today.' Instead of, 'What do I need from this person?' ask, 'How can I serve this person?'"

> You're basically asking yourself,
> 'How can I succeed today?' Instead, what if
> you were to ask, 'How can I serve today.'

"OK," I said. "I'll give it a try." (I was desperate.)

Though it seemed simplistic at first, the counselor's advice was a turning point for me in many ways. Although I at least philosophically believed in servant leadership and knew I wanted it from others, I now realize I wasn't practicing it. My own anxiety found me out. By consciously changing my question to "How can I serve?" I was freed up to help others get what they wanted—or needed. The paradigm shift led to a freer, more loving and peaceful me. As you might imagine, it produced much better outcomes too.

Paul was way ahead here. He challenged the Galatians to find their greatest freedom, not by indulging in pleasing themselves, but to *serve one another in love. . . . You, my brothers, were called to be free,* he said (Galatians 5:13). In actuality, the freest person was the one who could most consistently choose service. The servant was the leader. They found ways to help others succeed instead of using them for their own success. Jesus taught, *Whoever wants to become great among you must be your servant, and whoever wants to be first must be your slave* (Matthew 20:26-27).

One way to switch our mentality is to continually seek to add value to our customers, clients, and anyone we serve. By adding value, we actually seek to contribute to their success and well-being. We hold a perspective that says that when others are served above and beyond, they will not only become customers, but they'll be our biggest fans.

Of course this approach sounds naive and out of touch with reality in a dog-eat-dog economy. Healthy competition will certainly exist in a free market, but who of us would choose a dog-eat-dog approach if there were an approach that bestowed value on others? Those who offer the most value do well. At the end of the day, whether we made much profit or moved far ahead or not, we know that we served others. We made a difference in a life by doing things that added value to others. These people now have better information, better service, a healthier life, a nicer product.

Those who offer the most value do well.

Author Robert Quinn said, "We change the world by changing ourselves."[69] In reality, can we really change much else? If we want to produce extraordinary results, changing our own behavior can't be left to circumstance. We will need to invest in our own inner and outer growth. We will address our own selfness and find ways to transform destructive mindsets. We must see ourselves as ones who add value and not as needy takers. We'll be servants rather than self-seekers.

In our souls most of us want such service to be what we're about. We know it's a path of greater peace and deeper meaning. We're attracted to those who exhibit such servant qualities. In reality, they're the leaders we most admire. Yes, we've acted in selfish, self-centered ways before, but we know it didn't lead to a better life. Martin Luther King Jr. said, "Everyone has the power for greatness, not for fame but for greatness, because greatness is determined by service."[70] Such greatness comes at the expense of our egos and our longing to control.

Practically, it may come down to a willingness to start our days with a simple question: "How can I serve today?" Then really follow through. This may be the very thing that makes all the difference.

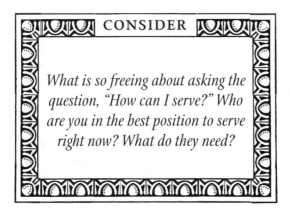

CONSIDER

What is so freeing about asking the question, "How can I serve?" Who are you in the best position to serve right now? What do they need?

32

Team with the Opposite Sex

Greet Priscilla and Aquila, my fellow workers in Christ Jesus.
ROMANS 16:3

Clear evidence exists in the New Testament that Paul actively teamed up with women. In a day and age where women were rarely seen as the equals of men, Paul cooperated with them and enlisted their help in his mission. He invited them to inner-circle opportunities. He valued their counsel and their gifts, and he recommended them to others.

It is clear from biblical evidence that Paul partnered with a least one married couple and several individual women. The couple, Priscilla and Aquila, served closely with Paul both in the business of tent-making and in the work of ministry. In the book of Romans we learn that this couple accompanied him on his journey to Syria. *They risked their lives for me,* he reported (Romans 16:3).

Paul then pointed to the work of a woman named Phoebe and described her as a *great help* to him. Writing to the church in Rome, he said, *I commend to you our sister Phoebe, a servant of the church in Cenchrea. I ask you to receive her in the Lord . . . and to give her any help she may need from you, for she has been a great help to many people, including me* (Romans 16:1-2). A few verses later, he mentions the name Junias, who most biblical scholars now agree was a woman. She was *outstanding among the apostles,* said Paul (Romans 16:7). Clearly, she participated with men as one of the apostles of her day, and Paul went further to say that among the apostles, she was *outstanding.*

This may already seem obvious to you, but enlisting the gifts and skills of the opposite sex can bring a wholeness to your endeavor, which you would miss if you didn't team with them. In the Book of Genesis, Adam started out working on his own. He cared for the Garden and gave names to all the animals; but paradise was less than perfect.

There was no complement to man, no counterpart, and God considered this a problem. *It is not good for the man to be alone,* said God. *I will make a helper suitable for him* (Genesis 2:18). So God caused man to fall into a deep sleep and formed a "completer" and "helpmeet" who could provide both the community Adam needed, as well as a sense of balance to his work. She's very similar and at the same time very different.

For too long, many workplaces, boards, and leadership structures have left out this very necessary balance. Men assumed that they had the complete perspective to run things. Boards and leadership teams were comprised of all males. Although women have always possessed essential skills and gifts, for the most part until recent times, they were left out or passed over. In 1970, Congresswoman Shirley Chisolm said, "Tremendous amounts of talent are being lost to our society just because that talent wears a skirt."[71]

For too long, many workplaces, boards, and leadership
structures have left out this very necessary balance.

I must admit that I waited too long to bring women into my leadership teams, and I really missed out. I continued to look for the right guy to fill a need or a slot, when what I needed to consider was the right *person*, regardless of gender. I created all-male boards and all-male committees. Yes, they functioned, but I am convinced they could have functioned even more effectively had I included women from the start.

One can't team with just any man or woman. The kind of partnerships we are talking about are like a marriage of sorts. Just like you don't necessarily marry the first person who comes along, when choosing a teammate, it's important to find the right person with the right skills, the right values, and the right disciplines. If you're a man, you are wise to seek out women with leadership skills. At the very least it would serve you well to seek out the female perspective on strategies as they relate to women. Yes, it's true. The best person to understand a woman is usually—this may come as a shock—a woman. Let's admit it men; in the past we thought women were just like us!

Women, the opposite holds true for you as well. If you're a female leader, seek out men who will serve with you. Their perspective can be invaluable to you just as yours can be to them. Find men who value your leadership skills and who recognize your call to your role.

If it's not possible to enlist someone of the opposite sex directly into a leadership team, then seek them out for input or to act as advisors. If you're a man, consider hiring a female consultant. Ask her, "What do women think of this? How might a mother perceive it? Does this relate well to a woman's taste? Are we connecting with women in our market? Which ones?" Or simply bring her in if she has the most knowledge on the subject, if she's the expert. Similarly women, consider bringing in a male consultant. His perspective may be just what you need to round out your board or team.

If it's not possible to enlist someone of the
opposite sex directly into a leadership team,
then seek them out for input or to act as advisors.

The secret is to work well with the opposite sex. Recognize the unique
vantage point they bring to the table. We were created to complete one
another. Take advantage of that complementary perspective, and don't
miss out.

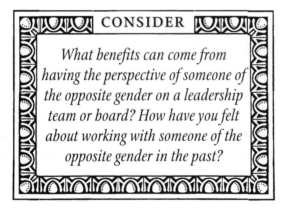

CONSIDER

*What benefits can come from
having the perspective of someone of
the opposite gender on a leadership
team or board? How have you felt
about working with someone of the
opposite gender in the past?*

33

Let People Go

Barnabus wanted to take John, also called Mark, with them, but Paul did not think it wise to take him, because he had deserted them.

ACT 15:37-38

Like getting a cavity filled, few of us take pleasure from letting people go. There are times we must let go of partnerships that don't work out. Whether employees, clients, sub-contractors, or suppliers, there's a time to hire and a time to fire. Perhaps the fit hasn't been right for them or for us, and it's time to cut the losses and go our separate ways. Maybe the arrangement looked promising at first, but we really didn't know the full story. They had expectations of us and we had expectations of them, either of which may not have been articulated. Now, it's time to make a change. Maybe the time has come to restructure, so they can use their gifts elsewhere.

Some of us tend to avoid conflict and end up letting things go too long. We fail to set up regular review systems or to pay the price to hold people accountable. We let things get sloppy before talking about the "dead moose on the table." Before things get to this point, however, we need to have an expectations conference or at least establish a more clearly agreed upon job description. But even if we implement these changes, too much water may have passed under the bridge; it may be time for an exit strategy.

The longer we let things go on, the harder solutions will become. Pent up feelings may erupt, or more damage may be done. Avoidance is rarely a good strategy in these cases. Things swept under the rug only fester and create bumps.

The longer we let things go on, the harder solutions will become.

Scholars still question whether Paul did the right thing by releasing John Mark and parting ways with Barnabus over the issue of John Mark's desertion in Pamphylia. Upon reading the biblical text, we can see that what arose wasn't a calm and businesslike meeting but a *sharp disagreement* (Acts 15:39). It was clearly not one of Paul's most shining leadership moments. Still, he made his decision and moved on. It didn't sink him or wreak havoc on the mission. Both parties went their separate ways, but they all remained committed to the mission. *Barnabus took Mark and sailed for Cyprus, but Paul chose Silas* (Acts 15:39-40).

Paul had the ability to hold people loosely. He loved them but didn't *need* them. He was okay whether they joined or didn't join. He was okay if they left and moved on. He didn't try to grab on and force the partnership to continue or prohibit Barnabus from going on without him. He didn't badmouth him once he left. He simply let go and moved on.

How willing are you to hold your expectations of others loosely? Whether partners, clients, or employees, do you have the ability to let them stay free? Can they move on without it sinking you? Can you let others go when the fit isn't right without seeing it as a failure or a character issue? Can you agree to disagree?

To avoid relationships that don't fit, it is most beneficial to clarify expectations up front. Put the expectations of both parties in writing. Seek to understand what they expect of you and what you can expect of them. It's a good idea to revisit your agreements regularly.

To avoid relationships that don't fit, it is most beneficial to clarify expectations up front.

Create an environment that enables others to succeed. If, on the other hand, they choose to bow out and move on, allow them to leave with their honor intact. There's nothing wrong with honestly admitting when the fit isn't right. If you can, share what you value in them and what they have brought to the relationship. Be sure to learn why the person is leaving, and seek to make right any wrongs.

If you initiate the parting, share what you consider the positive aspects of them joining the organization, but also let them know what fell short or why things didn't work out. Then, with as much blessing or severance as you can grant them, send them on their way—prayerfully and respectfully, wishing them well.

When others choose to move on, remember that you don't need their contribution to fulfill your mission. If gaps arise, there will be another to take the individual's spot. But let people be free, and allow yourself to be free. Hold others with an open hand and not a clenched fist, just as you would want to be held. Love and let go.

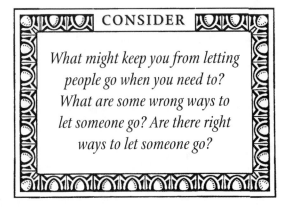

CONSIDER

What might keep you from letting people go when you need to? What are some wrong ways to let someone go? Are there right ways to let someone go?

34

Ask for the Order

Believe in the Lord Jesus, and you will be saved.

ACTS 16:31

I recently read a statistic stating that after explaining their products and services, more than 60 percent of the time, salespeople don't ask for the order.[72]

Paul certainly didn't fit this profile. He invited people to make a decision about what he presented—to believe, to accept, or to change their direction. He invited people to get involved, and they responded. They believed and were baptized. They joined the movement. They followed.

When the opportunity arose, Paul didn't shrink back from opening his mouth. *Believe in the Lord Jesus, and you will be saved,* he told the Philippian jailer (Acts 16:31). The jailer believed. In another situation, Paul boldly shared his own story with a powerful monarch, *King Agrippa, do you believe the prophets?* (Acts 26:27). King Agrippa was astonished by Paul's boldness, but chose to say no. Nonetheless, Paul did his job. He asked.

Most would agree that Paul had a sense of confidence both in himself and in God. He believed that God empowered him, stating, *I can do everything through him who gives me strength* (Philippians 4:13). When opportunities presented themselves, Paul was not one to say, "I'll pray about this and get back to you later." God gave him strength, and he took action. He challenged people. He spoke up.

When the time is right, how willing are you to ask? Do you move to ask a person to make a commitment, or do you shrink back and put it off?

When the time is right, how willing are you to ask? Do you move to ask a person to make a commitment, or do you shrink back and put it off?

For whatever reason, some give in to various excuses. "Oh, they'll never be interested," or "I wouldn't want to infringe upon them," or "I'm afraid they'll say no." Coach trainer Thomas Leonard calls it our "psycho block." It's the fear inside us that keeps us from taking the right next steps.[73]

As an entrepreneurial leader, taking the risk to ask for the order is part of your life. As the biblical principle states, *You do not have, because you do not ask* (James 4:2). You can move forward when you discern the self-defeating voices. It is essential for you to realize that when they say no to your product, opportunity, or idea, they're not rejecting you. They're rejecting whatever it is you are selling. You're just the messenger.

Sometimes when they say no or not now, it could be that it's not the right thing for them or they're not ready yet. Maybe you need to help them gain a better understanding so that they will see their need. Maybe it's not the right time. Maybe they need to struggle a little longer before they will be ready to realize they need what you have to offer.

Either way, it's not about you. It's okay to ask. In fact, if you don't ask, the chances of a connection are very low. And if they decline, you may learn some valuable things if you seek to understand their reasons. What's in their objection that may be valid? Maybe what you have to offer is not a good fit for them. In that case, they wouldn't be a suitable client anyway. You may need to stand back and look for the hidden blessing in the situation as we talked about in chapter 24.

Some people respond without an invitation; however, they are likely in a small minority. Most will wait until you ask them before they will make the decision. Even if you've hinted at it, they may not respond until you ask them directly.

Most will wait until you ask them before they will make the decision.

It may be as simple as asking, "Would you like to give this a try?" or "Would you like to buy one?" The common answers are yes and no. Sometimes maybe, which can mean they simply need more information. At least then you will know where you stand.

You may need to overcome some fears along the way, like the fear of being told no. Maybe you are under pressure because so much is resting on the person's response. Maybe you're afraid of rejection. Are you suffering from feelings of inferiority, thinking, *Who am I to think that this individual would buy from me?* Once you present your information, it's okay to go for it. Give people the opportunity to say yes. Ask. Put yourself out there. You never know, a yes may be only as far away as your invitation.

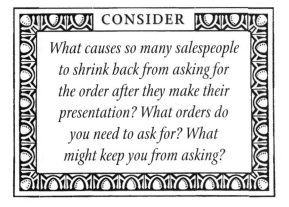

CONSIDER

What causes so many salespeople to shrink back from asking for the order after they make their presentation? What orders do you need to ask for? What might keep you from asking?

35

Believe in Destiny

He determined the times set for them and
the exact places where they should live.

ACTS 17:26

Paul didn't believe in coincidence. He believed in destiny. He believed the people in his path and the places in which he found himself were not a matter of chance crossing, but divine appointments. One who possessed a bigger plan than Paul could fathom determined them. Of the throngs of people in the world, each individual that was in Paul's life was there for a reason. Paul taught that God determined the exact places they should live. To the Corinthian church Paul said, *In fact God has arranged the parts in the body [of Christ], every one of them, just as he wanted them to be* (1 Corinthians 12:18).

It takes faith to believe in destiny. At times we need to suspend our calendars and our strategies in order to flow with an unplanned opportunity. We need to stop doing the tangible work in front of us and engage in something else. We realize much is happening around us that is beyond our control; we're part of a bigger picture. My belief is that the couple from England I reconnected with recently at my seminar and the Dutch woman who wanted to be on my mailing list were not there by chance. They were there for a reason. Can I know why? Maybe. Or maybe not.

This doesn't mean we abandon all plans and float helter-skelter, looking for coincidences and chance meetings. We don't quit day jobs and sleep in late. But we should always be open to something unexpected, be available to serendipity, realize that the most important meeting we attend in any day may not be one that's planned. The late author Henri Nouwen tells the story of a teacher at Notre Dame who once said, "I used to think that interruptions were killing my ministry. Then I came to see that the interruptions were my ministry."[74]

"I used to think that interruptions were
killing my ministry. Then I came to see
that the interruptions were my ministry."

Paul noticed a crippled man in a crowd in Lystra who wanted to be healed and *looked directly at him* (Acts 14:9). In other words he *noticed* the man; he wasn't too busy to notice. The result was a supernatural healing. With great fanfare, Paul went to the great city of Philippi with the potential for huge numbers to attend his messages, but something changed. Instead of Philippi, he journeyed to a river and met with a small gathering of women. We read, *One of those listening was a woman named Lydia, a dealer in purple. . . . The Lord opened her heart to respond to Paul's message* (Acts 16:14). His side trip might not have made the most sense, but it ended up being the encounter that launched his mission in Philippi!

From the clues given, it seems like this wealthy businesswoman became a catalyst for much of what happened to create the Philippian church. She persuaded Paul and his traveling companions to stay at her house. Paul didn't fret about his agenda changing. He recognized and embraced the spontaneous direction his trip had taken.

Destined appointments usually don't take much effort on our part. Instead, they require us to flow with them and not try to control the outcomes, staying open handed as we pay attention to the person before us. Encounters don't have to be difficult or feel like work to be effective. As Blaise Pascal wrote in his work *The Pensees,* "The strengths of a man's virtue must not be measured by his efforts but by his ordinary life."[75]

Maybe that impromptu phone call you've been thinking about making is a "prompting" you shouldn't avoid. You wonder, *Is this person coming to mind for a reason?* It may be time to find out. How about the billboard you can't get off your mind? Is there something you're supposed to consider? Sometimes it's most important to suspend what we're doing and just be present to what is going on around us.

A side benefit of such a belief in destiny is that you'll stop working so hard. Flexibility can cause you to relax more and have a sense of everything around you "working together for the common good." You start to see opportunities as gifts and chance meetings as significant in a larger plan. Possibly the best part of all is that your life becomes an adventure.

As you allow destiny to unfold your mission, you will discover a supernatural hand at work in the universe. You will find that when you're working according to the mission of your life, things seem to just happen. They aren't coincidences. Pay attention to those events. Allow yourself to be guided by a Purpose and a Hand bigger than yourself. Then watch to see what unfolds.

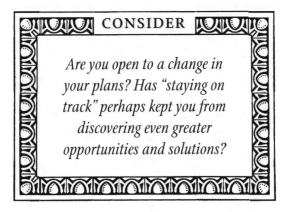

CONSIDER

Are you open to a change in your plans? Has "staying on track" perhaps kept you from discovering even greater opportunities and solutions?

36

Simplify

The entire law is summed up in a single command:
"Love your neighbor as yourself."

GALATIANS 5:14

Let's face it. Much of Paul's message and mission dealt with complex issues that were confusing for most people. Even today theologians spend lifetimes trying to understand concepts in the Bible, and they use peculiar words to describe Paul's teaching. They call it "Pauline Theology" and talk about his views of substitutionary atonement, justification, sanctification, ecclesiology, and eschatology.

I personally spent four years studying many of these subjects from professors with doctorates. They taught me how to parse Paul's verb forms and try to understand his meaning by reading the idioms of his days in Greece. Some of my professors gained doctorates by becoming experts in just one of Paul's letters. To accomplish this, they were privileged to study in renowned places like Tubigen and Oxford. As a pastor, I spent months teaching from Paul's individual letters, Philippians and Ephesians, for example. Sometimes I wondered if Paul had shown up during one of my sermons if he might have said, "What? That's not at all what I meant!"

Somehow, Paul learned how to articulate complex ideas and difficult concepts—and then simplify them. He spelled out what it meant and maybe even more importantly, what we should do upon hearing his message—the application. One of my professors used to say, "Simplify . . . simplify . . . simplify." Catholic author Henri Nouwen used to spend many hours seeking to make his writing simpler and more applicable. Today we would call it the KISS principle—Keep It Simple Stupid.

The KISS principle—Keep It Simple Stupid.

Paul knew the value of spelling it out for people. *The entire law is summed up in a single command: Love your neighbor as yourself* (Galatians 5:14). Many years later, theologian Søren Kierkegaard said all that really mattered was "the one thing."[76] Paul would likely know exactly what he meant and why most of us need to have things simplified.

Your mission has its complexities and underlying plans, strategies, justifications, and philosophy, but in simple terms, what are you doing? How can you simplify things to sixth-grade terms, so those who need to know can understand?

The hard work of good advertising is to take complex messages and make them simple and compelling, causing us to take action. Consider slogans by familiar corporations: G.E.—"We bring good things to light," "Ford Trucks: Built to Last," "Bounty: The Quicker Picker-Upper." There are countless others, but they all have one thing in common: they have managed to articulate what they do in very basic terms.

When I began to serve leaders as a coach, I wrestled to describe my function and how I could help them. After fumbling for a while, my own coach finally helped me come up with the simple description: "I act as a locksmith and work with you to unlock your potential." That one sentence helped make sense of something that seemed nebulous to many.

One company president I work with sought to describe why the concept of his office complex was worth the extra money for technology companies. He told me that some potential clients didn't understand why this complex was so unique. After some discussion, we came up with a simple analogy to describe what he did: "When coals are separated from each other, they quickly lose heat and go out. When they're together, they spur each other into a flame. That's what we do for small technology companies. They share resources, ideas, and equipment."

Another way to keep it simple is to have short, easy-to-understand goals. Keep them memorable and understandable. What are you trying to accomplish this week, this month, or this year? Try to articulate it in a brief word or phrase.

It's often easier to say more or write more than to keep it simple. Winston Churchill was noted to have said, "I wanted to write a short letter, but I didn't have the time."[77] There seems to be almost a homespun kind of simplicity to many effective leaders. They don't take themselves too seriously or try to complicate things. They don't speak over people's heads. Instead they reach the point clearly and concisely.

It's often easier to say more or write more than to keep it simple. Winston Churchill was noted to have said, "I wanted to write a short letter, but I didn't have the time."

I could probably say much more on this subject, but it's probably best to take this advice myself. Keep it simple. I'll stop there.

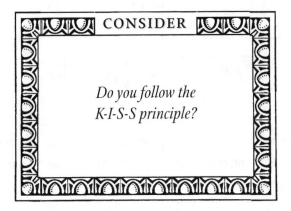

CONSIDER

Do you follow the
K-I-S-S principle?

37

Believe in Abundance

*To him who is able to do immeasurably more than all we ask
or imagine, according to his power that is at work in us.*

EPHESIANS 3:20

Robert Schuller, the pastor of the Crystal Cathedral Church in
California, was once asked by a young pastor how much he thought
God would provide for their growing church. Schuller challenged the
pastor to believe in supernatural abundance. "If you ask God to fill a
thimble," he said, "He will fill it. If you ask Him to fill a bucket, He will
fill it. If you bring him a barrel, He'll fill that too."[78] The young man
seeking counsel was Bill Hybels, founder and senior pastor of Willow
Creek Community Church. (Incidentally, God did indeed fill a large
barrel in South Barrington, Illinois!)

Other leaders have been inspired by this idea. Why not dare to ask for
the barrel?

Paul believed that the universe was filled with abundant supply. He
asked for huge barrelfuls, and he received them. His vision included
cities, regions, continents, and people groups. Writing to the Ephesian
church, Paul articulated his belief that God was *able to do immeasurably
more than all we ask or imagine* (Ephesians 3:20). In other words, God's

capacity to meet needs far exceeds anything we anticipate or even request by prayer. Paul said this divine work took place *according to his power that is at work within us* (Ephesians 3:20).

According to Webster's Dictionary, the word *supernatural* includes "actions or happenings preceded by the existence of forces above the natural." Supernatural happenings "violate what are assumed to be natural laws." They do the seemingly impossible.

Speaking to a group of philosophers in Athens, Paul challenged them to see God as bigger and more supernatural than they had previously pictured. He told them, *The God who made the world and everything in it . . . does not live in temples built by hands. . . . For in him we live and move and have our being* (Acts 17:24-28). His point was that we can't place limits around a limitless and life-giving God. He might have said to them, "Look up at the sky. Look at the trees, the oceans, and the birds. Look in the mirror. Stop limiting what is limitless."

For the entrepreneurial leader, the supernatural abundance mentality means overcoming our propensity toward natural scarcity. We look around and wonder where the things we need can possibly come from. We question our ability to rise above our challenges of cash flow and market competition. We wonder if we have what it takes and if we can really accomplish what we set out to do. Too often we limit our perspective by focusing on the here and now.

For the entrepreneurial leader, the supernatural abundance mentality means overcoming our propensity toward natural scarcity.

I believe Paul would challenge us with the words of J. B. Phillips: "Your God's too small."[79] You're looking at what is instead of using your faith to see what can be. You may need to recalibrate your perspective and renew your faith. Take an inventory of all the seemingly impossible things that have come about. Look where you are now and where you came from. You might find it helpful to read some biographies of others who have held on to big dreams and persevered despite difficult setbacks. Take time to look up and see the limitless potential. Why not dare ask for the barrel to be filled, although you have no idea where it might come from?

When I lived in Boston, I spent many lonely and discouraged nights outside our suburban townhouse staring up at the stars. I contemplated the enormity of the sky and thought about all the billions and billions of stars I had learned about in my college astronomy classes. I would think about the psalm of King David which said, *When I consider your heavens, the work of your fingers, the moon and the stars, which you have set in place, what is man that you are mindful of him, the son of man that you care for him?* (Psalm 8:3-4). *If the universe is that vast,* I would think to myself, *surely God has the power to work through me.*

A belief in supernatural abundance trusts that there are many out there who fit into your master plan, but you haven't yet encountered them. Some you encounter will be interested right away. There are those out there who want to help in some way. During an especially difficult and seemingly unsuccessful time in Paul's life, God himself reminded him of supernatural abundance. One night in a vision, God said, *Do not be afraid; keep on speaking, do not be silent. For I am with you, and no one is going to attack and harm you, because I have many people in this city* (Acts 18:9-10).

Some will think you're nuts. They will wonder why you're asking for a barrelful instead of just a thimbleful. They think you should be satisfied with the thimbleful. They will wonder why you're on this crazy adventure and why you haven't settled down. Cast aside their discouraging remarks and look instead to God's promise of supernatural abundance.

Some will think you're nuts. They will wonder why you're asking for a barrelful instead of just a thimbleful. They think you should be satisfied with the thimbleful.

The Bible is full of God's words inviting us to ask, seek, and desire. Jesus taught, *Ask and it will be given to you; seek and you will find; knock and the door will be opened to you* (Matthew 7:7). In Psalms we read, *Delight yourself in the LORD and he will give you the desires of your heart* (Psalm 37:4). In Psalms we read of one seeking aid and finding supernatural abundance, *I lift up my eyes to the hills—where does my help come from? My help comes from the LORD, the Maker of heaven and earth. He will not let your foot slip—he who watches over you will not slumber* (Psalm 121:1-3).

There are questions you will need to answer for yourself. Do you believe in supernatural abundance? Do you have a big view of God and a big view of the universe? Do you believe the heavens and the earth are vast—or that we live on one overcrowded blue ball on which you're just one small person? Do you believe that you are in the right place to do what you've been chosen to do? That God will supply all your needs of people, resources, ideas, and money? Are you willing to decide now to seek so you will find and ask in order to receive?

It may be that this is your time. The heavens will open up and pour out the resources as you dare to dream big and believe. Draw forth all of your courage and dare to believe in a big God.

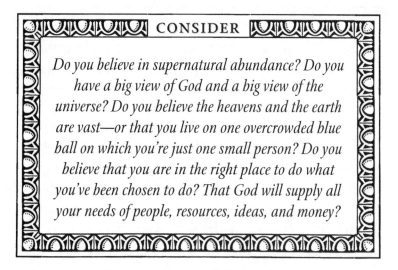

CONSIDER

Do you believe in supernatural abundance? Do you have a big view of God and a big view of the universe? Do you believe the heavens and the earth are vast—or that you live on one overcrowded blue ball on which you're just one small person? Do you believe that you are in the right place to do what you've been chosen to do? That God will supply all your needs of people, resources, ideas, and money?

38

Keep Your Eyes on the Prize

Run in such a way as to get the prize.

1 CORINTHIANS 9:24

What does it look like to live with no regrets? What would happen if you continually pushed yourself out of comfort zones and focused on the potential? Like a runner, you exert concentrated energy, honed skill, and fervent intensity to win the race marked *for you.* You aim not to simply cross the line or receive the bronze. Instead, you go for the gold.

Paul saw himself as such an athlete, determined to win the grand prize. He wanted the gold and refused to settle for anything less. In the words of author Oswald Chambers, Paul put forth his "utmost for His [God's] highest."[80] He said, *There is in store for me the crown of righteousness, which the Lord, the righteous Judge, will award to me on that day* (2 Timothy 4:8). Using athletic metaphors, he says, *I press on toward the goal to win the prize* (Philippians 3:14). And, *I do not run like a man running aimlessly; I do not fight like a man beating the air. No, I beat my body and make it my slave so that after I have preached to others, I myself will not be disqualified for the prize* (1 Corinthians 9:26-27).

Entrepreneurial leaders must learn how to keep going when things get tough. In his book *Man's Search for Meaning,* Nazi-death-camp

survivor Victor Frankl articulated the concept that those who overcome the most challenging circumstances usually possess a meaningful goal or desire that pulls them through. They have something
bigger that keeps them going: a vision, a calling, a loved one, faith, a
goal to accomplish. They believe something greater is worth living
for and that enduring even the most difficult circumstances imagin-
able is worthwhile.[81]

The first step is to know what prize you're running after. What would
success look like for you? Like Paul, some entrepreneurial leaders prize
the heavenly reward. They seek to honor God through what they do
and how they do it. They seek to leave a legacy.

When businessman Bob Muzikowski moved into inner-city Chicago
with a desire to start a baseball league for less fortunate kids, there was
much standing in the way of his prize. He had a hard time earning
credibility or even finding a field to play on. Yet his goal was to give
kids some of the things he never had as a kid. "There was no sense of
right and wrong, no truth in my life as a kid," he says. With that in
mind, he set out to provide a healthy alternative to gangs, heroin, and
hopelessness. The league is now thriving and is supported by patrons
from around the country.[82]

Other entrepreneurial leaders place great value on the accumulation of
knowledge and understanding. Their endeavors involve extensive
research and investigation into the way things work or to invent new
technologies. They seek ways to improve things that are already being
done. Others want to unlock secrets that will lead to a cure for termi-
nal illnesses. Perhaps for them, their prize would be the eradication of
cancer from the earth. Some accept lower salaries, long hours, and
often work in obscurity to win their prize.

Others want a financial return on their risk and investment. One man I know is purchasing a car wash with a goal of using the money as a way to educate his children. For others, philanthropy may be the end goal.

As you define and record your ultimate prize, it will pull you forward. It will enable you to remain enthusiastic on those days you feel like throwing in the towel.

As you define and record your ultimate prize, it will pull you forward. It will enable you to remain enthusiastic on those days you feel like throwing in the towel.

It is vital to keep your eyes on the prize, but it is just as essential to keep your eyes *off* of distractions. These alternate prizes vie for attention. They present themselves as smoother routes, better bets, and more lucrative propositions. You receive job offers just when things seem most sour in your endeavor. Someone seeks to recruit you to their mission. Well-meaning folks try to help, by attempting to rescue you from paying the price of your own ambitions. They think they're being helpful by encouraging you to play it safe.

As any athlete knows, when you're training, you must watch your diet and make sacrifices, while others rest, eat, and spend. Others on the sidelines wonder why you're working so hard and when you're going to quit. They wonder why you'd trade benefit packages, paid vacations, or free weekends for the life you've chosen.

Keeping your eye on the prize also means getting by the quitting points. These will test your willingness to strain forward when you feel like throwing in the towel. You wonder if you're progressing as fast as you should. The finish line seems like an eternity away. Emotionally, you feel fatigued, discouraged, and spread thin. You wonder if reaching your goal is possible or pointless.

In Paul's metaphor the focused athlete presses on despite distractions and quitting points. He overcomes the distractions from within and without. He recalls the upside potential: the crown, the cash reward, and the victor's stand. He keeps in mind the windfall that awaits him if he endures. The gain is worth the pain.

Paul never apologized for his own belief that he would one day be rewarded for his risks and his work. He believed that one day he would stand before God himself and receive the ultimate paycheck."He would hear God say, "Well done, good and faithful servant." Such a reward clearly pulled Paul on when things were stacked against him.

Days before his death, Leonardo da Vinci wrote, "As a well-spent day brings happy sleep, so does a well-used life bring a happy death."[83] Though da Vinci certainly suffered in his life, he realized that his goal had been great understanding and knowledge. His life had allowed him to share with others his insights into mathematics, philosophy, the arts, and anatomy.

Days before his death, Leonardo da Vinci wrote,
"As a well-spent day brings happy sleep,
so does a well-used life bring a happy death."

Near the end of his life Paul wrote, *I have fought the good fight, I have finished the race, I have kept the faith* (2 Timothy 4:7). Refusing to look back or complain, he took hold of the mission, and he kept going, keeping his eyes firmly on the prize.

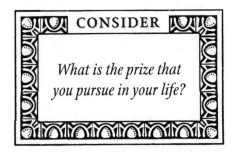

CONSIDER

What is the prize that you pursue in your life?

END NOTES

1. Keith Hammonds in "Soul Proprietor," *Fast Company Magazine*, (Issue 37, August 2000) p. 154.

2. Garth Brooks and Victoria Shaw, "The River," from *Ropin the Wind*, (Capitol Records, ASIN B00005176B, 1991).

3. *Dynamic Spiritual Leadership*, J. Oswald Sanders (Grand Rapids: Discovery House Publishers, 1984), p. 15.

4. *Wild at Heart*, John Eldredge (Nashville: Thomas Nelson, 2001), p. 12.

5. *Dynamic Spiritual Leadership*, p. 21.

6. From lecture by Ken Blanchard at Faithworks Conference, Cambridge, MA, 1998.

7. *The Call*, Os Guiness (Nashville: Word Publishing, 1998), p. 32.

8. Ibid.

9. *Let Your Life Speak*, Parker Palmer (San Francisco: Jossey-Bass Publishers, 2000), p. 3.

10. *Creating You & Company*, William Bridges (Reading, Massachusetts: Addison-Wesley Books; 1997), p. 27.

11. *Letters from the Desert*, Carlo Corretto (New York: Orbis Books), 1972, p. X.

12. Ibid. p.73.

13. *Run with the Horses*, Eugene Peterson, (Colorado Springs, Intervarsity Press, 1983).

14. Talk given at the Foundation Conference, San Diego, CA, September 21, 2001.

15. Article by Kris Maher, *Boston Globe*, June 29, 2001 (Career Journal: *The Jungle of Recruitment, Pay and Getting Ahead.*)

16. *Let Your Life Speak*, p. 16.

17. *The Call* p. 1.

18. *The Soul of a Business*, Tom Chappell (New York: Bantam Books), 1993, p. xv.

19. Ibid. p. xii.

20. *Inspiring Quotations*, Dwight L. Moody, as quoted by Albert M. Wells Jr. (Colorado Springs: Waterbrook Press, 1991), p. 172.

21. Albert Schweitzer as quoted in *Simpson's Contemporary Quotations*, James B. Simpson, (New York: Houghton Mifflin Company, 1988) #4269.

22. *Braveheart*, Directed by Mel Gibson (Paramount Pictures, 1995).

23. William Wallace, as quoted in the film *Braveheart*.

24. *If You Want to Walk on the Water, You'll Have to Get Out of the Boat*, John Ortberg (Grand Rapids: Zondervan Publishing, 2001).

25. Source Unknown.

26. Ken Blanchard in talk given at Faithworks Conference in Boston, MA, March, 1998.

27. Cited in *Flow: The Psychology of Optimal Experience*, by Mikaly Csikszentmihalyi (New York: Harper Collins, 1991).

28. *Life Compass: How to Find and Fulfill Your Unique Purpose*, Dr. Steven Lake (unpublished manuscript).

[29] *Whistling in the Dark: A Doubters Dictionary,* Frederick Buechner,(Harper San Francisco, 1993).

[30] Words from "I'll Tell You Now," *Sacred Hunger,* Ian Morgan Cron (Nashville: Moon Belly Music, 2001).

[31] Oscar Wilde as cited in *Quest for the Soul,* Robert L. Wise, (Nasheville: Thomas Nelson Publishers, 1996), p. 32.

[32] *Emotional Intelligence,* Daniel Goleman (New York: Bantam Books, 1995), p. 56.

[33] Oscar Wilde quoted in *Quest for the Soul: Our Search for Deeper Meaning,* Robert L. Wise, (Nasheville, Thomas Nelson Publishers, 1996), p. 32.

[34] *Now and Then,* Frederick Buechner (San Francisco: Harper San Francisco 1991) p.4.

[35] Taken from USA Weekend.com and adapted from *Sabbath: Remembering the Sacred Rhythm of Rest and Delight,* by Wayne Muller. (New York: Bantam Books, 1999 by Wayne Muller).

[36] Gordon MacDonald in talk given at Conference sponsored by Intervarsity, MIT, April, 1998.

[37] *Making All Things New: An Invitation to the Spiritual Life,* Henri Nouwen (San Francisco: Harper and Row Publishers, 1981), p. 72.

[38] *The Twelve Steps: A Spiritual Journey,* author: "Friends in Recovery" (RPI, 1994) p. 124.

[39] From a radio show with Dr. Paul Meier of the Meier Clinics, February 2002.

[40] *The Inner World of Choices,* Frances Wickes (Boston: Sigo Press, 1988).

[41] *Innovation and Entrepreneurship,* Peter Drucker (New York: Harper and Row Publishers 1985.), p. 30.

[42] *Odyssey,* John Scully (New York: Harper & Row, 1987), p. 90.

[43] *Managing by Values,* Ken Blanchard and Michael O'Connor, (San Francisco: Berrett-Koehler Publishers, 1997) p. 23.

[44] *The Soul of the Firm,* William Pollard, (Grand Rapids: Zondervan Publishing, 2000).

[45] *Paul: A Critical Life,* Jerome Murphy O'Connor (New York: Oxford University Press, 1996).

[46] *Christian Coaching: Helping Others Turn Potential into Reality,* Gary Collins (Colorado Springs: Navpress, 2001), p. 14.

[47] Ibid., p. 37.

[48] *The Company of the Committed,* Elton Trueblood (New York: Harper Collins, 1979).

[49] *Visionary Leadership,* Burt Nanus (San Francisco: Jossey-Bass, 1995) p. 26.

[50] *Principle-Centered Leadership,* Stephen R. Covey (New York: Summit Books 1991), p. 45.

[51] *The Active Life: A Spirituality of Work, Creativity, and Caring,* Parker Palmer (San Francisco: Jossey-Bass Publishers, 1990) p. 8.

[52] *The Twentieth Century New Testament,* Leon Tucker, (Kregel Publications, 1983).

[53] *Lead On,* John Haggai (Waco, Texas: Word Books, 1986) p. 106.

[54] Michael Card, "The Things We Leave Behind," from *Poiema* (Sparrow Records, ASIN B000005KX7, 1994).

[55] *The Life You've Always Wanted,* John Ortberg (Grand Rapids: Zondervan, 1997).

[56] *Pain: the Gift No One Wants,* Philip Yancey and Paul Brand, (Grand Rapids: Zondervan Publishing House, 1997).

[57] *Leading from the Inside Out: The Art of Self-Leadership*, Samuel D. Rima (Grand Rapids: Baker Books, 2000), p. 61.

[58] *The Responsible Entrepreneur*, Craig Hall (Franklin Lakes, NJ, Carreer Press, 2001), p.21.

[59] *The Path*, Laurie Beth Jones (New York: Hyperion Books, 1998). p. xvii.

[60] *Fast Company* "Operation-Leadership" Eli Cohen and Noel Tichy, (September 1999, #27) p. 278.

[61] Ibid., p. 279.

[62] Ibid., p. 279.

[63] *Receiving the Day*, Dorothy C. Bass (San Francisco: Jossey- Bass Publishers, 2000), p. 3.

[64] *First Things First*, Stephen Covey ((New York: Simon & Schuster, 1994), p. 75.

[65] *Coach Yourself to Success*, Talaine Miedaner (New York: McGraw-Hill/Contemporary Books, 2000).

[66] *Ten Natural Laws of Successful Time and Life Management*, Hyrum Smith (New York: Warner Books, 1994), p. 3.

[67] From *The 7 Habits of Highly Effective People*, Stephen R. Covey (New York: Simon & Schuster, 1989), p. 261.

[68] *Stop Selling, Start Partnering*, Larry Wilson (New York: John Wiley and Sons, 1995).

[69] *Change the World: How Ordinary People Can Accomplish Extraordinary Results*, Robert E. Quinn (San Francisco: Jossey-Bass Inc. 2000), p. 19.

[70] Martin Luther Kings Jr. as quoted on Brainyquote.com.

[71] Shirley Chisolm as quoted in collection of Famous Quotes at Tawjihe.com.

[72] *Focus*, Mark Hanson and Jack Canfield (Deerfield Beach, Florida: Health Communications, 2000).

[73] Thomas Leonard from lecture presented at Coachville Conference, Las Vegas, NV, March 2002.

[74] *Reaching Out*, Henri J. M. Nouwen, (New York: Image Books/Doubleday, 1986) p. 52.

[75] *The Pensees* (as quoted in *Mindy on Fire*), Blaise Pascal – collection edited by Dr. James Houston, (Minneapolis: Bethany House Publishers, 1997).

[76] From *Provocations: The Spiritual Writings of Soren Kierkegaard*, (Farmington, Pennsylvania: The Plough Publishing House, 1999), p. 3.

[77] Winston Churchill as quoted on Brainyquote.com.

[78] Conversation with Robert Schuller as quoted by Bill Hybels in Leadership Conference Talk, 1994.

[79] *Your God's Too Small*, J. B. Phillips, (Carmichael, California: Touchstone Books, reprint 1997).

[80] *My Utmost for His Highest*, Oswald Chambers, (New York: Dodd, Mead and Company, 1935).

[81] *Man's Search for Meaning*, Viktor Frankl (New York: Washington Square Press, 1997).

[82] From John Ortberg's interview with Bob Muzikowski, Willow Creek Community Church, February, 2002.

[83] As quoted in *If Success is a Game, These Are the Rules*, Cherie Carter-Scott (New York: Broadway Books, 2000), p. 7.

ABOUT THE AUTHOR

JEFF CALIGUIRE is the President of Unlocking People Inc. and works as an encourager, consultant and coach with entrepreneurial business and non-profit leaders throughout the country and overseas.

Caliguire is a graduate of Cornell University, Dallas Theological Seminary. He is a voracious student of startups, coaching, and the spiritual life. In the 1990's he served as the co-founder and Senior Pastor of Beacon Community Church and Operation Beacon Street in the Boston area, founded and directed Boston Sports Fellowship, and served as chaplain of the New England Revolution. He also worked with DOMA Group hosting "Leadership Refineries" for leaders in New England.

As a business and personal coach, Caliguire has developed tools and coaching techniques to help leaders "unlock their potential in leadership, legacy, and life." He also facilitates personal and group retreats on life calling, entrepreneurial leadership, and legacy planning.

He and his wife Mindy are co-authors of *Write for Your Soul, the Why's and How's of Journaling* and the creators of SoulCare.com. and UnlockingPeople.com. He and Mindy now make their home in Algonquin, Illinois and are the parents of Jeffrey, Jonathan, and Joshua (the "J-Team").

Additional copies of *The Leadership Secrets of Saint Paul*
are available from your local bookstore.

If you have enjoyed this book, or if it has impacted your life,
we would like to hear from you.

Please contact us at:

RiverOak Publishing

Department E

P.O. Box 55388

Tulsa, Oklahoma 74155

Or by e-mail at *info@honorbooks.com*